Police Recruitment and Retention for the New Millennium

The State of Knowledge

Jeremy M. Wilson, Erin Dalton, Charles Scheer,
Clifford A. Grammich

Supported by the U.S. Department of Justice's
Office of Community Oriented Policing Services

RAND Center on Quality Policing

A RAND INFRASTRUCTURE, SAFETY, AND ENVIRONMENT CENTER

This project was supported by Cooperative Agreement 2007CKWXK005 awarded by the Office of Community Oriented Policing Services, U.S. Department of Justice. The opinions, findings, and conclusions or recommendations contained herein are those of the authors and do not necessarily represent the official position of the U.S. Department of Justice. References to specific companies, products, or services should not be considered an endorsement of the product by the authors or the U.S. Department of Justice. Rather, the references are illustrations to supplement discussion of the issues. This project was conducted under the auspices of the RAND Center on Quality Policing (CQP), part of the Safety and Justice Program within RAND Infrastructure, Safety, and Environment (ISE).

Library of Congress Cataloging-in-Publication Data

Police recruitment and retention for the new millennium : the state of knowledge / Jeremy M. Wilson.

p. cm.

Includes bibliographical references.

ISBN 978-0-8330-5017-5 (pbk. : alk. paper)

1. Police—Recruiting—United States. 2. Police—United States—Personnel management. 3. Employee retention—United States. I. Wilson, Jeremy M., 1974-

HV8141.P5933 2010
363.2'20973—dc22

2010027437

Published 2010 by the RAND Corporation
1776 Main Street, P.O. Box 2138, Santa Monica, CA 90407-2138
1200 South Hayes Street, Arlington, VA 22202-5050
4570 Fifth Avenue, Suite 600, Pittsburgh, PA 15213-2665
RAND URL: http://www.rand.org/
To order RAND documents or to obtain additional information, contact
Distribution Services: Telephone: (310) 451-7002;
Fax: (310) 451-6915; Email: order@rand.org

Preface

Maintaining the police workforce level is one of the most salient challenges facing law enforcement today. In the long run, both the supply of and demand for qualified officers are changing in a time of increasing attrition, expanding law-enforcement responsibilities, and decreasing resources. These contribute to the difficulties that many agencies report in creating a workforce that represents the demographics of their communities, that is committed to providing its employees the opportunity for long-term police careers, and that effectively implements community policing.

These difficulties, perhaps surprisingly, have persisted through recent recessionary times and may become more challenging as the economy improves. Department resources have continued to decrease and responsibilities to increase, with agencies being asked to do more police work with fewer resources. Some agencies report staffing shortages (a small number still claim continuing drops in applications). Others question whether the long-term commitment of applicants and current officers will persist in times of economic improvement.

To help address these challenges and provide lessons for the law-enforcement community, this monograph does not offer any new data but rather summarizes for police practitioners lessons on recruiting and retaining diverse, effective workforces. It provides a means for local officials to identify what has been tried elsewhere and what might be applicable in their own communities. It is a broad analysis of issues confronting many agencies and how these have developed over time. Each agency will face unique circumstances that it must consider in workforce planning; this monograph can provide guidance on relevant lessons learned elsewhere. Focusing specifically on recruitment and retention, this guide does not address other key personnel planning issues, such as specific ways of determining staffing need, allocation of staffing resources, distribution of staff attributes and qualities, and opportunity costs and implications of implementing recruiting and retention strategies on other parts of the organization, which are also important to development of an effective, efficient workforce. Challenges might vary by agency, especially by local conditions confronting each agency.

This monograph builds on other resources the RAND Center on Quality Policing has developed with the support of the U.S. Department of Justice's Office of Community Oriented Policing Services, particularly a Web-based recruitment and retention clearinghouse (see RAND Corporation, 2010). This monograph also builds on a national summit of police recruitment and retention, also supported by the Office of Community Oriented Policing Services, held at RAND in June 2008 (for the report, see J. Wilson and Grammich, 2009a; for the briefings, see COPS, undated[a]). It should be of interest to policymakers and researchers concerned with understanding and responding to police personnel challenges.

The RAND Center on Quality Policing provides research and analysis on contemporary police practice and policy. By determining what practices are most cost-effective and results-oriented, the center's work helps law-enforcement agencies across the United States make better operational decisions and consistently perform at their best. For more information on the center, visit its website, http://cqp.rand.org/, or contact the center's director, Greg Ridgeway, at Greg_Ridgeway@rand.org. For more information on this monograph or the Recruitment and Retention Clearinghouse, write to Jeremy Wilson, the lead author and director of the Recruitment and Retention Clearinghouse, at jwilson@msu.edu.

Contents

Figures

Tables

Summary

Maintaining the police workforce level is continually one of the greatest challenges facing law-enforcement agencies. One indication of this challenge is the recent appropriation of $1 billion to the federal Office of Community Oriented Policing Services (COPS) to help stabilize law-enforcement positions. The program received more than 7,000 applications requesting more than $8 billion to support nearly 40,000 sworn-officer positions.

To help address these challenges and provide lessons for the law-enforcement community, the COPS office provided support to the RAND Center on Quality Policing to compile information on promising practices for police recruitment and retention. These are available at the Recruitment and Retention Clearinghouse website (RAND Corporation, 2010). This monograph summarizes for police practitioners lessons evident in these materials on maintaining diverse, effective workforce levels.

A Metaphor for Police Staffing Challenges

Diminishing sources of recruitment, increasing causes for attrition, and broadening police responsibilities all shape questions of workforce supply and demand. To conceptualize and delineate the distinct forces at work, we use the metaphor of a bucket (Figure S.1).

In this metaphor, the size of the bucket represents the absolute need for police officers. The water level, which rises and falls with accession and attrition over time, frequently does not fill the bucket because the demand for officers exceeds the ability to meet it due to resource or

Figure S.1
The Bucket Metaphor and Demand for Police Officers

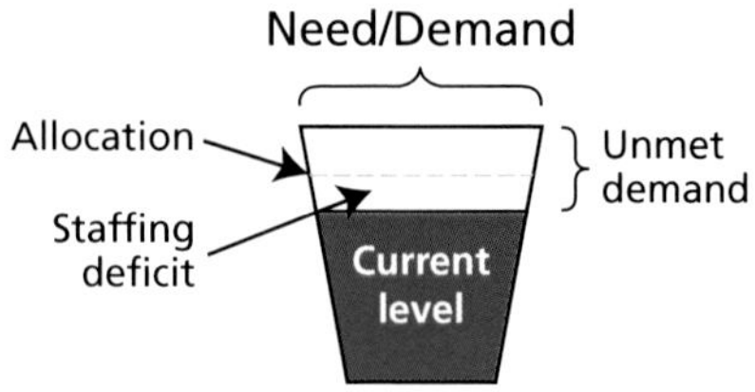

RAND *MG959-S.1*

other limitations. The difference between the need and the current level represents unmet demand for officers. The authorized or allocated level of officers, representing the number of officers for which an agency is budgeted, is usually between the current level of officers and demand for them and is politically determined by such variables as workload, service orientation, and available resources.

Three forces can affect the bucket and the "water" in it. First, officers might be "leaked" through a hole in the bucket caused by attrition. Attrition can result from several sources. Budget crises might cause jurisdictions to reduce their number of officers. Organizational characteristics might become unappealing to officers who decide to pursue work elsewhere. A pending wave of baby-boom generation retirements threatens to reduce experience levels of police departments across the nation. Increasing numbers of military call-ups are requiring more officers for longer periods of time on nation-building and other military duties. Finally, younger generations of workers might be more likely than older ones to change careers to find the work they like best. Understanding these and other sources of retention problems is critically important. It is far more costly and time-consuming to recruit an officer than to retain one. Reducing retention problems can alleviate much of the need for recruiting.

Second, new officers might be less likely to flow from the "faucet" of supply into the bucket than they once were. Changing generational preferences mean that not only might younger workers be more likely to change careers once entering policing—they might be less likely to enter policing at all. Furthermore, increasing levels of illicit drug use, of obesity, and of debt have led to decreases in the qualified applicant pool (Derby, 2008). Expanded skill requirements for police work further constrict the pool of qualified applicants. While many applicants (e.g., the college-educated) can meet these requirements, there is also competition from other sources for them. Just as budget crises can lead to increased attrition, so also can they lead to reduced salaries and benefit packages that are less likely to attract candidates to policing. Departments might also fail to take full advantage of electronic media in their recruiting efforts.

Third, the capacity of the bucket is expanding as police work broadens, creating the demand for more "water" to fill it. The adoption of community policing has broadened the duties of police agencies, which increases the number of functions police undertake, especially for larger departments. Increased emphasis on homeland security has also widened the responsibilities of local police officers, increasing the demand for them. Finally, as a result of globalization, technological advancement, and greater awareness, the scope of crime the law-enforcement community must now address continues to grow. In sum, local police roles have expanded to include not only benign order-maintenance duties, such as answering noise complaints and solving neighborhood disputes, to new, occasionally militaristic roles, such as counterterrorism, information-sharing, and immigration enforcement.

Filling the Bucket: How Can Police Agencies Improve Recruitment and Retention?

There is little that local police agencies can do to limit the scope of their work and the subsequent demand for officers. Nevertheless, there are some practices they can adopt to improve recruitment and retention and, hence, their ability to meet the demand for services.

First, planning, analysis (including analysis of demographic trends), and surveys and interviews with officers about job satisfaction can help agencies understand their prospects for attracting and keeping officers. Second, agencies can reduce turnover by offering realistic job previews to candidates and requiring contracts with new employees. Third, agencies can attract and retain candidates by enhancing compensation and other benefits. Fourth, agencies can increase retention through greater employee engagement, including efforts to increase employee input in decisionmaking and other evaluation and feedback opportunities. Improving organizational effectiveness through better hiring and management practices can improve the agency's image not only with employees but also with the community.

Research on recruitment and retention is evolving and still has some significant gaps. Local agencies will need to identify what has been learned elsewhere and apply the lessons to their specific problems. This guide can provide a means for local officials to identify what has been tried elsewhere and what might be applicable to their own situations.

Acknowledgments

We would like to thank the COPS office for providing support to create this resource. Additionally, Matthew Lysakowski and Matthew Scheider provided useful comments throughout its development. We appreciate the informal feedback provided to us by numerous police practitioners about the issues we raise, and the formal comments on drafts provided to us by our peer reviewers, Nelson Lim and Bruce Taylor. Lisa Bernard and RAND's publication team improved the readability of the monograph by offering effective editorial and production support. We thank all of these individuals (and those we do not identify specifically) for significantly enhancing the final product.

Abbreviations

CBR	chemical, biological, and radiological
COPS	Community Oriented Policing Services
FBI	Federal Bureau of Investigation
LAPD	Los Angeles Police Department
LEAA	Law Enforcement Assistance Administration
PCSO	Pinal County Sheriff's Office
PERF	Police Executive Research Forum
RSS	really simple syndication
SWAT	special weapons and tactics

CHAPTER ONE

Introduction

In early 2009, Congress appropriated $1 billion for the U.S. Department of Justice, Office of Community Oriented Policing Services (COPS), for the COPS Hiring Recovery Program to help stabilize law-enforcement positions. The COPS office received a staggering 7,272 applications for this program requesting $8.3 billion to support more than 39,000 sworn-officer positions throughout the United States (COPS, 2009a). These statistics highlight two glaring facts: The need for police officers is great, yet the ability to support the officers is limited.

While recent recessionary conditions have mitigated some of these problems for some agencies, others report staffing shortages (a few even report continuing drops in applications), and still others report concern that they might not be able to retain candidates once economic conditions improve. Police agencies generally have not applied known and demonstrated tenets of personnel management to their occupation. Researchers have provided few empirical lessons about what works and what does not in recruiting and retaining officers, leaving gaps on topics of concern to law-enforcement officials. Law-enforcement agencies typically lack the time, resources, and expertise to collect and assess data and to develop lessons for their own personnel planning needs.

Objective and Approach

This monograph synthesizes research about promising practices for recruitment and retention, focusing on empirical studies. We explain what is known about various strategies, drawing heavily on the policing literature but supplementing that by highlighting the effectiveness of these strategies in the military, medicine, education, business, and other professions. This monograph does not present original research but can help local officials, each of whom will face unique circumstances, identify what has been tried elsewhere and might be applicable to their own communities. While, as noted, some gaps remain in the literature, and some of the literature is based more on anecdote than empirical research, we trust that this review can help local officials understand what is and is not known. The resources summarized in this monograph are drawn from those we have compiled for the Recruitment and Retention Clearinghouse website (RAND Corporation, 2010).

Outline

In the next chapter, we introduce the recruiting and retention challenges confronting police organizations, using the metaphor of a bucket to delineate the issues and circumstances involved in understanding the problem and changes in the organizational context of policing. We use the bucket metaphor in subsequent chapters to illustrate how staffing challenges arise and how police organizations can respond to them. Chapter Three summarizes what is known about retaining personnel. Chapter Four highlights lessons about recruiting personnel. We choose to discuss retention first to highlight three facts: It is far more costly and time-consuming to recruit an officer than to retain one; improving retention can alleviate the need to recruit; and retention issues are frequently overshadowed by discourse about recruitment. The final chapter summarizes the most-promising recruitment and retention practices based on current research.

CHAPTER TWO

The Dynamic Police Staffing Challenge: The Bucket Metaphor

Diminishing sources of recruitment, increasing causes for attrition, and broadening police responsibilities all shape questions of workforce supply and demand. To conceptualize and delineate the distinct forces at work, we use the metaphor of a bucket (Figure 2.1). In this metaphor, the size of the bucket represents the absolute need or demand for police officers, which will vary by agency based on workload determinants and service objectives.

The Bucket Metaphor and Demand for Police Officers

The water inside the bucket represents the current level of police strength. The water level varies over time with accession and attrition and frequently does not fill the bucket because the demand for officers exceeds

Figure 2.1
The Bucket Metaphor and Demand for Police Officers

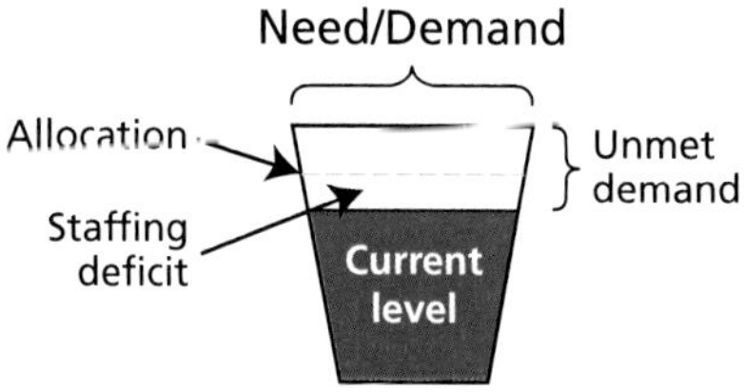

RAND *MG959-2.1*

the ability to meet it (due to resource and other limitations). The difference between the need and the current level represents the true unmet demand for police officers.

Usually somewhere between the current level of officers and the demand for them is the authorized or allocated level of officers. This represents the number of officers for which an agency is budgeted. A somewhat artificial threshold, the allocation level is politically determined by such variables as workload, service orientation, and available resources.

The staffing deficit is the difference between the allocated and actual levels of police strength. Actual staffing levels rarely rise above allocated levels, although this can occur when an agency is building up capacity in anticipation of attrition. The bucket metaphor visually illustrates that an agency can, in fact, be understaffed when it is operating with its full complement of allocated officers.

Three forces can affect the bucket and the amount of water in it. Officers might be "leaked" through a "hole" caused by attrition. New officers might be less likely to "flow" from the "faucet" of new supply. The bucket might expand as police work broadens. These issues might not affect every agency equally or in the same magnitude, but there is evidence of them affecting at least some agencies both in the short and long terms. Every agency has its own unique circumstances that must be considered in workforce planning.

The Hole in the Bucket Is Widening

Much of the difficulty police agencies face in maintaining their workforce levels is a product of attrition. To be sure, attrition can be positive, as when a department replaces retiring officers with younger, more-skilled ones, or when it loses those who are not committed to being effective, high-performing officers. Nevertheless, attrition can be a problem when it occurs in waves, such as with past hiring booms ultimately resulting in large proportions of staff retiring within a short time of one another. This causes the attrition hole in the bucket to widen, making it increasingly difficult to maintain the actual level of officers, or the water in the bucket.

Figure 2.2 highlights some contributors to the widening of the

Figure 2.2
Attrition Is Widening the Hole

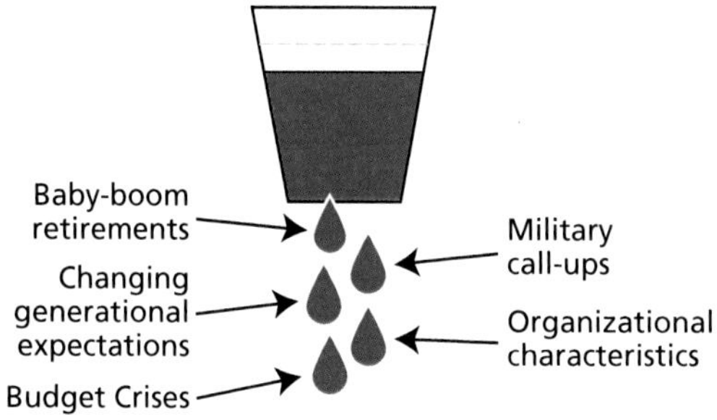

RAND *MG959-2.2*

hole in the bucket: baby-boom generation retirements, changing generational preferences, budget crises, military call-ups, and organizational characteristics.

Baby-Boom Generation Retirements

Baby-boom generation officers on the cusp of retirement are the greatest pending concern. Officers of this generation are beginning to retire, and the number of retirements is likely to grow considerably in the next few years as the number of officers eligible for retirement increases significantly.

This pending wave of retirements is already affecting departments. In the early 2000s, New York City faced an exodus of officers who had 20 or more years of service, prompting the department to offer retention bonuses and incentives ("NYPD Facing a Flood of 20-and-Out Retirees," 2000). By the end of the decade, facing the additional challenge of paying pensions that the city budget could not afford, New York Mayor Michael Bloomberg proposed abolishing the "20-and-out" rule in his 2009 budget as a way to end the out-migration (Bloomberg, 2009). In Chicago, an early retirement option is expected to increase, from just more than 500 to nearly 900, the deficit of officers below the overall authorized level of 13,500, a problem exacerbated by the department's need to wait for federal funding before scheduling new academy classes (Spielman, 2009). Likewise, the proportion of retirement-eligible officers in Edmonton, Alberta, is expected to increase from less than 10 percent in October 2009 to nearly 20 percent by 2014; this challenge is expected to recur in 2030 as those hired through recent aggressive recruiting become eligible to retire (Edmonton police official, 2009).

The recent downturn in the economy might delay some of these retirements and expand the applicant pool, but retirement requirements and pension reforms will eventually affect all departments and, perhaps, threaten services. In Vallejo, California, for example, recent police retirements coupled with the economic downturn have sparked community concern about the viability of public services (Wolf and Rohrs, 2008). In Boston, changes in pension benefits partially attributable to the economic crisis have led to increased retirement applications across several municipal services (Levenson and Slack, 2009). In Macon, Georgia, early retirement options might debilitate an already thin police force (Womack, 2009). All these trends are widening the hole in the metaphorical bucket, making it difficult to replenish the supply of officers, and even creating a "brain drain" among the most experienced.

Similar trends are evident in other fields, a result both of impending retirements of older workers and of changes in life and career goals of younger ones (Edwards, 2007; Losey, 2005; Graig and Paganelli, 2000). Yet, these trends appear to have affected retention more strongly in policing than in other fields (Taylor et al., 2006; Orrick, 2008a). Increases in law-enforcement turnover have also resulted from police salaries that are lower than private-sector ones, competition with military recruiters, a negative public perception of law enforcement, and lack of interest in policing by younger Americans entering the work force (Jordan et al., 2009; Pomfret, 2006; Egan, 2005; Tulgan, 2000). An increasing number of police are leaving the service prematurely, compounding the macro social trends and their bearing on the police profession (Jordan et al., 2009). Of greater concern are the reportedly low levels of career and organizational commitment of police officers in the United States (Frost, 2006), similar to that in Australia and New Zealand (Lynch and Tuckey, 2004). Low organizational commitment has been seen as an antecedent of a decision to voluntarily leave an organization (Frost, 2006). Yet, other researchers—using evidence that points to fallacies in Bureau of Labor statistics, increasing workforce productivity, baby boomers' willingness to work longer than previous generations, the influx of younger generations into the workforce, and increases in life expectancy—contend that attrition and turnover are not as chronic a problem as social trends would indicate (Edwards, 2007; Graig and Paganelli, 2000; Pikitalis and Morgan, 2003).

Police studies of attrition demonstrate constancy in turnover across multiple locales. Rather than decreasing as a result of turnover, in California, between 1985 and 2005, the number of police officers increased from 63,694 to 84,443 (Switzer, 2006). Transfers to other agencies were fairly stable over the same period, between 3 and 5 percent annually. A survey of 205 North Carolina sheriffs' departments of varying size found steady turnover (12.7 percent) and vacancy (5.5 percent) rates, with 28.6 percent of agencies surveyed noting either a significant or slight increase in turnover rates (Yearwood, 2003).

Retention changes with economic conditions. In times of relative prosperity, other careers and positions might pull officers away from police work with higher salaries and easier work. In times of economic decline, officers might be less likely to leave departments due to concerns about better job security, but departments might be forced to lay off or furlough employees in the wake of budget cuts.

Changing Generational Preferences and Expectations

Retention also changes with generational preferences. Younger generations of workers might have less organizational commitment than older ones, with many even changing careers (Wheeler, 2008; Twenge and Campbell, 2008).

The changing nature of work has had a pronounced effect on attrition in policing. The movement toward knowledge work, currently transforming career paths, might be reshaping career expectations in law enforcement. The evolution of "boundary-less" careers has required workers to move between employers to gain knowledge and competencies that will enhance expertise and employability (Lynch and Tuckey, 2004). This shift heightens the challenges that police organizations face in retention and succession planning. In Australia and New Zealand, researchers found that police organizations are no longer limited to their traditional crime-detection and law-enforcement functions (Dupont, 2003). They are being reshaped into, among other things, knowledge brokers, social-service referrers, or problem solvers. This transformation might intensify turnover in law enforcement due to unanticipated realities and unfulfilled expectations.

Younger workers might also change jobs more often than older ones, especially in metropolitan areas with diverse economies, in an effort to find the work they like best (Wheeler, 2008; Twenge and Campbell, 2008). This creates difficulties for police departments, which invest considerable time and resources in selecting and training officers, only to have them leave after a short term.

Budget Crises

Decreasing financial support to cover officer salaries has contributed to widening the hole in the bucket through resulting limits both on funding positions and on providing competitive salaries and benefits. Two extreme cases of the effects this can have on retention are evident in New Orleans and San Diego. In New Orleans, many police officers relocating their families to Houston after Hurricane Katrina joined the department there or another elsewhere that offered higher pay and benefits than New Orleans had (see box, facing page). In San Diego, uncompetitive wages and salary freezes led many police officers to seek better opportunities elsewhere, including a lead detective with 21 years on the force who applied for a patrol position in the neighboring community of Chula Vista (Manolatos, 2006).

The recent economic downturn has punctuated this problem. Many communities are struggling to cover the expenses of their police workforces and have responded with tactics ranging from hiring freezes and cancellations of academy classes to furloughs and even layoffs. Officials in Prospect Heights, Illinois, even closed the police station to the public and assigned the police chief and command staff to patrol shifts (J. Byrne, 2009). Those agencies that can hire report a spike in applications and improved ability to hire officers, but some practitioners have raised concerns about the willingness of those who are now pursuing positions to commit to a long-term policing career (DeLord, 2009). The Macon, Georgia, police chief warned that an early retirement option might drain his department of more-experienced and knowledgeable officers (Womack, 2009). Johnstown, Pennsylvania, struggles to replace

Rebuilding After a Crisis and a Catastrophe: New Orleans

As it did on most other elements of the city, Hurricane Katrina had a profound effect on the New Orleans Police Department. In the storm's aftermath, Warren Riley (2008), superintendent of the department, told a RAND summit on recruitment and retention, most officers were homeless, their families had been displaced, and, in some cases, they had to deal with the loss of loved ones. Often, Riley said, "[o]fficers were stranded in flooded police stations, trapped in attics, and in some cases, on rooftops."

The wounds the department suffered proved to be deep and lasting for some time after the storm. "The media coverage following the storm was extensive and often not very positive when it came to the Police Department," Riley said. "It made [the department] appear to be a losing team." The subsequent bleeding to the department would last for some time. From the time of the hurricane until the end of 2005, the department would have 165 separations, with 147 related to officer actions or lack of performance following the storm. Losses would continue past the immediate aftermath of the storm, particularly among lower ranks. Not until 2007 would department hiring exceed separations (Figure 2.3).

By then, separations had claimed one-third of the prestorm force. Complicating matters for the department was the fact that, even before the storm, its staffing level was nearly 8 percent below its allocated level. A year after the storm, its staffing level was nearly 12 percent below its allocated level, even though the budgeted allocation of officers had decreased by nearly one-sixth (Table 2.1).

Although the storm had wounded the department deeply, in some cases, it might have been more a trigger for departures than a cause of them. Over time, New Orleans police salaries and benefits had come to lag those of many other cities (Rostker, Hix, and Wilson, 2007; J. Wilson, Rostker, and Hix, 2008). For nearly all ranks, RAND researchers found that New Orleans' officer pay lagged that

Figure 2.3
New Orleans Police Department Hires and Separations, 2004 to 2007

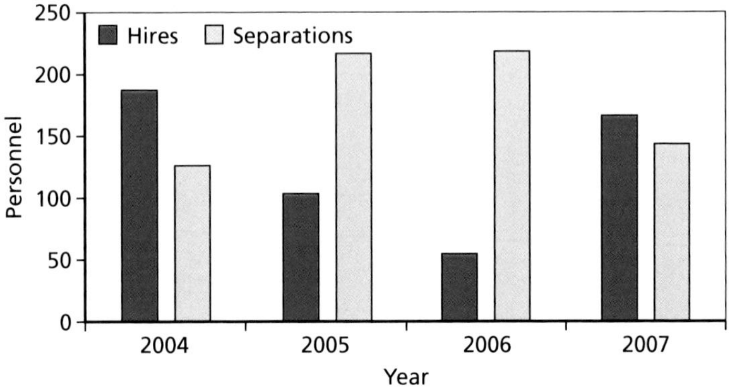

RAND *MG959-2.3*

of Houston, where many residents relocated at least temporarily after the storm. Officers above the rank of sergeant could earn about $30,000 more per year in Houston than in New Orleans (Table 2.2).

Budget constraints the city faced limited its options for improving recruitment and retention. Fortunately, RAND researchers found, there were several low-cost initiatives the city could take to make its compensation packages more attractive to new officers. While New Orleans police salaries were low, their pensions were generous. Shifting money from pensions to salaries could, in the near term and at no net cost, make the department more attractive to new recruits. Likewise, RAND researchers suggested increasing the frequency of promotional boards, passing only enough officers to fill expected vacancies, to allow talented officers to rise through the ranks more quickly and to create a climate of continual learning.

For the medium term, RAND researchers suggested two low-cost options: converting appropriate jobs from officers to civilians and developing proactive recruiting efforts, such as after-school and

Table 2.1
Budgeted and Actual New Orleans Police Officer Levels, Before and After Hurricane Katrina

Level	August 2005	October 2006	Change (%)
Budgeted	1,885	1,600	–15
Actual	1,742	1,421	–18

SOURCE: Stephanie M. Landry, New Orleans Police Department, as cited in Rostker, Hix, and Wilson (2007).

NOTE: Data for 2005 are current as of August 21, 2005. Data for 2006 are current as of October 24, 2006.

Table 2.2
New Orleans and Houston Police Department Salary Comparison, 2006

	Annual Base Salary Without Benefits ($)		
		Houston	
Rank	New Orleans	Minimum	Maximum
Police recruit	30,732	29,164[a]	
Police officer 1[b]	33,111	36,022	50,039
Police officer 2	34,797		
Police officer 3	36,570		55,235
Police officer 4	38,433	51,114	
Police sergeant	42,449	61,784	67,362
Police lieutenant	45,734	69,354	75,606
Police captain	53,750	75,421	86,613
Police major	58,633		

SOURCES: Stephanie M. Landry, New Orleans Police Department, as cited in Rostker, Hix, and Wilson (2007); City of Houston (undated).

[a] Recruits with a bachelor's degree earned up to $33,784 during academy and field training.

[b] A police officer 1 with a bachelor's degree in Houston earns more than $47,000 the first year after the probationary period, including an equipment allowance, shift/weekend pay, and bilingual pay. After one year of service, a New Orleans officer receives $3,600 in annual state supplemental pay. All New Orleans officers also receive an annual uniform allowance of $500.

summer employment for students interested in police work. Much of the recruiting work done by officers comprised recruiting those who had already volunteered and using the Internet and other tools to conduct background checks, tasks that civilian specialists could perform. For the long term, RAND researchers suggested offering housing to officers as an incentive for a commitment to years of service.

The city government acted quickly to implement many of the recommendations. "The mayor," Riley said, "and the city council . . . immediately bought into it, and it was smooth sailing from there." State law prohibited shifting pension resources to salaries, but the city still substantially increased officer pay and devised several education incentives. These recommendations helped cut department attrition, which averaged 11 officers per month before Katrina, to five officers per month.

experienced command staff on an already "depleted roster" (Faher, 2009).

A pattern is emerging: Agencies are increasingly offering early retirements to save costs and trim budgets, but the same budgets do not allow for hiring high-quality candidates—or any candidates at all—to replace those leaving. Limited resources have resulted not just in fewer positions but in attrition of officers from existing positions.

Military Call-Ups

Military call-ups represent another leak in the bucket. The United States has become increasingly involved in nation-building and peacekeeping missions (Dobbins et al., 2003; Jones et al., 2005; J. Wilson and Grammich, 2009b). The most recent examples of this include Afghanistan and Iraq. This causes the hole in the police staffing bucket to widen because many police officers serve as military reservists and have been called to active duty. During the 12-month period ending June 30, 2003, 21 percent of local police departments and more than 94 percent of agencies serving a population of at least 100,000 had full-time sworn personnel who were called up as full-time military reservists, with call-ups averaging three officers per department and ranging from one to 74 (Hickman and Reaves, 2006a). Such call-ups pose not just manpower but fiscal challenges; federal law requires that health benefits of these officers be maintained and their positions held until they return (Hickman, 2006).

Organizational Characteristics

Organizational characteristics can also affect attrition. Officers can choose to leave a department for a number of organization-related reasons, including the characteristics of their immediate supervisor, lack of career growth, unmet job expectations, inadequate feedback, insufficient recognition, or lack of training (Orrick, 2008a, 2008b; J. Wilson and Grammich, 2009a).

The Faucet (Supply) Is Tightening

Just as trends in attrition are making it difficult to retain police officers, the supply of qualified potential officers might be diminishing. That is, the supply faucet might be tightening (see Figure 2.4). Among contributors to this phenomenon are a general decrease in the qualified applicant pool, changing generational preferences, increased competition, expanded skill requirements, uncompetitive benefits, and organizational characteristics.

Decrease in Qualified Applicant Pool

As noted earlier, the generations replacing the baby-boomers now retiring are smaller. Exacerbating this problem are cohorts of young persons who do not meet the minimum requirements for becoming a sworn officer. Raymond et al. (2005) contend that it is becoming more difficult for the general population to meet minimum qualifications, such as a clean criminal record, little to no drug use, good physical health, and financial stability. Several key statistics support their claim:

- About half of all 12th-graders report having smoked marijuana, and one in four has used some illicit drug *other* than marijuana by the end of the 12th grade, levels of prevalence that are above those of the early 1990s (Johnston et al., 2008).
- Over the past three decades, the obesity rate has more than doubled for adolescents 12 to 19 years of age and has more than tripled for children ages 6–11 (Sturm et al., 2007).
- From 1992 to 2001, credit-card debt among Americans 18 to 24 years of age rose 104 percent to an average of nearly $3,000 per person (in 2001 dollars); the average indebted youth spends almost 30 percent of his or her income on debt maintenance (Draut and Silva, 2004). Younger generations, from which police departments would normally draw recruits, have higher amounts of debt than youths of previous decades (Draut, 2008). In some departments, outstanding debt can disqualify applicants, as it is interpreted as an indicator of bad judgment and a proclivity toward corruption.

Figure 2.4
The Shrinking Supply Is Reducing the Flow

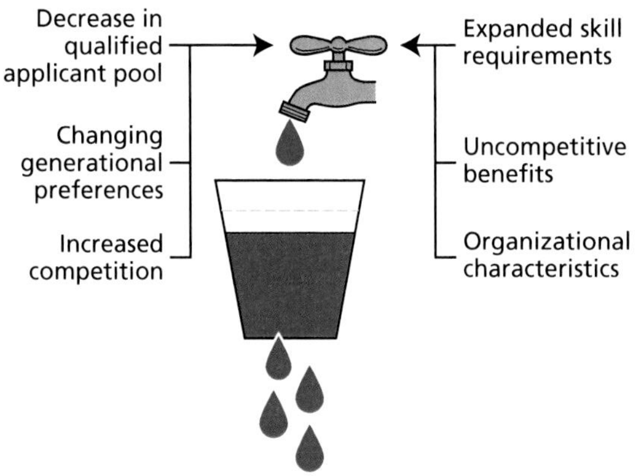

RAND *MG959-2.4*

Education trends matter too. In the past decade, the percentage of persons 25 to 29 years of age holding college degrees has remained virtually unchanged (Planty et al., 2008). Yet, the length of time to complete a degree has increased as the number of enrollees who complete their degree has decreased (Bound, Lovenheim, and Turner, 2007; Dynarski, 2005). These trends and the increasing costs of college can affect a graduate's career choice. An educated worker might meet law enforcement's increasing education standards but also has more job prospects, in turn making recruiting them into police work more competitive (Bound, Lovenheim, and Turner, 2007).

Changing Generational Preferences

The militaristic nature of police work, with its emphasis on hierarchy and formality, and the sacrifices that officers must make, from maintaining certain appearances (e.g., no beards or tattoos) to erratic schedules and long shifts, to placing themselves in harm's way, also likely discourage applicants. This same cultural shift has driven military propensity downward since the early 1980s and is compounded in younger generations as realities of military structure conflict with differing youth attitudes about the nature of work (Bowyer, 2007; DoD, 2003; M. Wilson et al., 2000). Moreover, changes in generational values regarding off-duty life have been seen as affecting recruiting (Brand, 1999), whereas the flexibility and emotional control sought by younger generations appears inconsistent with traditional paramilitary police environments (Harrison, 2007; Pew Research Center for the People and the Press, 2007). Less than half of American youths consider a police department or agency a "desirable" or "acceptable" place to work—more than those who view military service that way but fewer than those who view corporations, schools, or other government agencies that way (Sackett and Mavor, 2003). Furthermore, those entering the workforce today expect to have more-rapid advancement opportunities (J. Wilson and Grammich, 2009a) and to have a better balance between work and family (Scrivner, 2008). The youngest generation of workers has shown marked preferences toward extrinsic work values, such as prestige, changing tasks, social and cognitive aspects of work, and flexibility (Lawsson, 2009; Lyons, Duxbury, and Higgins, 2005). Many of these career expectations cannot be met in law enforcement.

Increased Competition

As noted earlier, local police agencies look to fill their ranks from a subset of the population that meets minimum qualifications, including a clean criminal record and good physical health. Nevertheless, they are not alone in searching for such candidates. The military, federal and state police agencies, private security firms, and other first-responder agencies recruit similar individuals, and opportunities with them have grown, particularly since the September 2001 terrorist attacks against the United States. The expansion of a security-industrial complex since the attacks has funneled money and personnel into increased private security positions (De Rugy, 2006; Kondrasuk, 2004), spurred demand for fire protection (Frawley, 2006), and stimulated national efforts and capital for security and defense contracting (Makinen, 2002). Military enlistments have increased, particularly among more-educated recruits (Kane, 2005). As a result, the labor market for such public services has become much more competitive. The greater compensation and benefits that other public service agencies can offer exacerbate the problem of competition for local police (Raymond et al., 2005; Rostker, Hix, and Wilson, 2007).

Although recent economic conditions seem to have relieved some competition for applicants, local police agencies still compete for many of the same recruits, particularly as they lure officers and potential recruits away from sister agencies and communities. In recent years, agencies have launched several incentives to attract officers, ranging from signing bonuses and moving expenses to health-club memberships and mortgage discount programs. They have also sought recruits hundreds or even thousands of miles away. In the 12-month period preceding June 2008, the Metropolitan Police Department in Washington, D.C., conducted recruiting trips to Fort Campbell and Fort Knox in Kentucky; Camp Lejeune, North Carolina; Albany, New York; Columbus, Ohio; Tidewater, Virginia; and Oak Creek, Wisconsin (Lanier, 2008). The Arlington County Police Department in Virginia sought recruits as far away as Puerto Rico, albeit with little success (see box, next page).

Expanded Skill Requirements

As in other industries (Rich, 2010), the changing nature of police work might also restrict the flow of eligible recruits. Police agencies face growing, more-complex problems in increasingly diverse communities, and policing work has become much more community-oriented. Such changes expand the skills required of police officers. Officers must now be able to work closely with different people, including being able to communicate, collaborate, and interact with a diverse set of stakeholders; have strong analytical, problem-solving, critical and strategic thinking, and technology skills; and be culturally competent (Miller, 2008; Raymond et al., 2005; Scrivner, 2006, 2008; J. Wilson and Grammich, 2009a). Scrivner (2008) also notes the need for officers to focus on service, values, multiple dimensions of performance (not just arrests), and outcomes. These changes call for recruitment efforts to be even more selective, thereby reducing the supply of qualified candidates.

Uncompetitive Benefits

Just as budget crises can widen the hole in the bucket, so too can they tighten the faucet. A key way in which law enforcement limits its supply of qualified applicants is by offering prospective candidates uncompetitive wages and benefit packages (which, as noted earlier, can also contribute to turnover). Officer salaries are not on par with the institutions with

Recruiting Among Competitors: Arlington County (Virginia) Police Department

When M. Douglas Scott became chief of the Arlington County Police Department, he found a department below its authorized strength of more than 350 officers (Scott, 2008). It was also facing an attrition rate of 10 percent per year. There were several reasons for this. In addition to the usual lures away, such as other employment or a return to school, the department, because it is located near the heart of the Washington metropolitan area, must compete with federal law-enforcement agencies in addition to neighboring agencies. The department also has an older force, with about one in seven currently serving also eligible for retirement. Complicating its recruiting efforts, Scott said, was a requirement of 60 college credit hours for new hires, with no waiver for military or other police service.

To maintain its numbers and increase its diversity—minority officers comprise 22 percent of the force and female officers 17 percent—the department has tried a variety of strategies. Among the more successful ones have been partnering with local criminal-justice programs, administering monthly exams, offering recruitment bonuses to employees, establishing a recruiting team, and developing recruitment efforts and websites. Some efforts, such as outreach to the Washington-area gay community, were controversial among some residents but not county leaders. Other efforts have been less successful, including a recruiting trip to Puerto Rico, job fairs far removed from the jurisdiction, a cadet program, and venues, such as parades and county fairs, not designed for recruitment. Successful retention initiatives have included increasing salary and retirement benefits. As a result of these efforts, the department was able to reach its authorized strength of 366 officers in 2006, 2007, and 2008.

which it competes for personnel. In 2003, the average entry-level starting salary was $35,500 for local police officers (Hickman and Reaves, 2006a) and $32,200 for deputies (Hickman and Reaves, 2006b). According to 2008 Bureau of Labor Statistics data, mean annual wages for all local police and sheriffs' patrol officers, at $52,480 per year, appear competitive with other public service occupations (such as firefighters and correctional officers), but they lag behind other possible professional occupations, such as physical therapists ($74,410 per year), physical- and social-science occupations ($64,280), landscape architects ($64,000), electrical engineers ($85,350), computer-science occupations ($74,500), and construction management ($89,770) (BLS, 2009).

In the past decade, according to Bureau of Labor Statistics figures, benefits and compensation costs were 51.4 percent higher for public than private employees, a figure that had increased steadily throughout the decade (McDonnell, 2002, 2005, 2008). But, looking closer at the discrepancy, wage and work differentials between careers in state and local government (which includes other public service professions) were the main source of the gap: Unionization rates and health-care program participation were seen as driving the discrepancy (McDonnell, 2008). Yet, the perception persists among upper-level police management that the reactive nature of salary and benefit improvements has resulted in a reduced ability to compete with private employment, which is viewed as providing a more attractive lifestyle (Domash, 2002).

Organizational Characteristics

Other organizational characteristics can also limit the supply of prospective qualified officers. The image of law enforcement as a career or of a particular agency, residency policies, length and complexity of the hiring process, and opportunities for advancement and special assignments are just some of the organizational factors that can influence interest in law enforcement (J. Wilson and Grammich, 2009a). Many of these organizational obstacles might affect minority candidates disproportionately (Wright, 2009). All create additional difficulties for police agencies and can change over time.

The Bucket (Demand) Is Expanding

While the staffing-loss hole in the bucket is widening from increased attrition and the flow replenishing it is shrinking from a reduced supply of qualified officers, the demand for officers is increasing the size of the bucket (see Figure 2.5). Without remedy, this serves to exacerbate the true unmet demand for police service (Figure 2.1).

The increasing demand for police officers largely originates from an expansion of their responsibilities. This is perhaps most vividly apparent regarding their roles in community policing, homeland security, and emerging crimes.

Community Policing

The adoption of community policing has broadened the duties of police agencies. In the past two decades, most police agencies have embraced some form of community policing (Maguire and Mastrofski, 2000; J. Wilson, 2006; Zhao, Lovrich, and Thurman, 1999). Since 1995, the COPS office (undated [b]), which is the federal agency tasked with advancing community policing, has invested $12.4 billion in community policing, enabling more than 13,000 state, local, and tribal agencies to hire more than 117,000 police officers and deputies. Fifty-eight percent of all local police departments, employing 82 percent of all officers, used full-time community policing officers during 2003, as did 51 percent of all sheriffs' offices, employing 70 percent of all deputies (Hickman and Reaves, 2006a, 2006b).

Community policing increases the number of functions police undertake, particularly for larger departments. Hickman and Reaves (2006a) found that most police agencies in jurisdictions of at least 25,000 residents work with citizen groups to develop community policing strategies, with four-fifths of those in jurisdictions of at least 100,000 having citizen police academies. Such proactive activities require time and resources in addition to those needed for traditional police responsibilities, such as maintaining law and order, preventing crime, and enforcing traffic regulations. In Oakland, California, for example, this required a ten-year, multimillion-dollar voter initiative to address community policing, violence prevention, and fire and paramedic services (see box, facing page).

Hiring for Community Needs: Oakland, California

The Oakland Police Department has traditionally faced a hire-and-freeze cycle, under which the department would hire when able but would see its staff dwindle during a hiring freeze (Poulson, 2008). In the early 2000s, for example, the department hired enough officers to boost its number of officers to 740 but, under a hiring freeze, saw this dwindle to 680.

This cycle changed in the wake of an increase in overall violence and in homicide specifically (J. Wilson, Cox, et al., 2007; J. Wilson and Cox, 2008). In 2004, Oakland voters passed the Violence Prevention and Public Safety Act, or Measure Y. This required the city to invest $19 million annually in violence prevention and community policing.

The sudden new demand for officers created difficulties for the department. For example, the community policing component of Measure Y alone required the department to hire at least 63 new officers. Further complicating department hiring was a consent decree requiring personnel for internal affairs, evolving policing requirements, and an ineffective shift schedule resulting in absenteeism rates as high as 40 percent for patrol officers.

Oakland's mayor ultimately sought to boost the department to 803 officers. This required the department to recruit and train 342 officers in just two years (both for new positions and to replace retiring officers). To do so, the department launched several recruitment, training, and retention initiatives. It launched a $1 million saturation advertising campaign, as well as a website, provided regular email updates to applicants, and streamlined its process so that it could hire a candidate passing a background examination within three weeks. It accepted candidates from other, unaffiliated academies. It paid $1,000 to officers who recruited and mentored a new recruit through the first few months on the job. It also boosted pay and adopted a new shift schedule calling for seven 12-hour shifts in a two-week period. As of the end of June 2010, 776 officers work for the department, but 80 of them have received layoff notices as the Oakland City Council attempts to manage a $30.5-million budget deficit (Kuruvila, 2010).

Agencies have sought to meet increased demand in several ways. Some agencies might delay police responses and cut special units, while others rely on cameras and other technologies to do the jobs that absent officers would normally fulfill (C. Fischer, 2009; Wiegler, 2008). The Lower Manhattan Security Initiative, which will blanket the city of New York with video cameras, has coincided with widespread attrition in the New York City Police Department, which has no pending plans to fund or hire additional officers (Winston, 2009).

Homeland Security

Increased emphasis on homeland security has also widened the responsibilities of local police officers, increasing the demand for them. Since the September 11, 2001, terrorist attacks against the United States, local police have been asked to perform additional patrol and surveillance,

Figure 2.5
Expanding Duties Increase the Demand for Police Officers

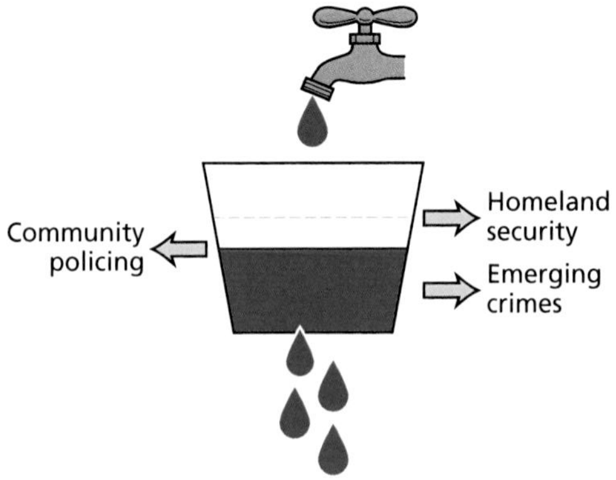

RAND *MG959-2.5*

gather and analyze counterterrorism intelligence, conduct risk and threat assessments, participate in various task forces, coordinate and communicate with other agencies, undergo new training and exercises, construct and contribute to fusion centers, formulate new policies, and update mutual-aid agreements and response plans for chemical, biological, and radiological (CBR)–related incidents (Davis et al., 2006; Raymond et al., 2005; K. Riley, Treverton, et al., 2005).

Homeland security duties for local police have also included an expanded role in immigration enforcement. As K. Riley, Treverton, et al. (2005) explain, before the September 11, 2001, attacks, many departments had explicit policies not to arrest and detain someone whose only crime concerned immigration status. Federal policy has since sought more participation of local agencies in immigration enforcement, although some are resisting this. Congressional authorization in 1996 of local agencies to act in immigration-enforcement capacities has also pushed smaller agencies into roles of a more global nature (Khashu and Malina, 2009).

Emerging Crimes

As a result of globalization, technological advancement, and greater awareness, the scope of crime the law-enforcement community must now address continues to grow. Over the past decade, police agencies have had to respond to emerging crimes, such as human trafficking, identity theft, cybercrime, and fraud, and take on roles, such as counterterrorism and internal security, usually reserved for the military (Kraska, 2007). Human-trafficking task forces have gained increasing worldwide attention as a local response to the global problem of trafficking in persons; such a strategy relies heavily on international cooperation, information-sharing, and a reconsideration of the local role of police (U.S. Department of State, 2009). Cybercrime and the related problems of intellectual-property theft and fraud are likely to increase, requiring local agencies to train officers to counter this new and evolving threat (FBI, 2008). In sum, local police roles evolved through the community policing era to include benign order-maintenance duties, such as answering noise complaints and solving neighborhood disputes, to new, occasionally militaristic roles, including counterterrorism, information-sharing, and immigration enforcement (Kraska, 2007).

The Weakened Economy

Recent economic changes have had mixed effects on police staffing. In this time of rising unemployment, agencies with the resources to hire officers have been inundated by applications, thereby permitting greater selectivity and, potentially, a more qualified applicant pool. A wave of applicants for six positions in Ventura, California, came from industries as diverse as software and mortgage (Scheibe, 2009). Agencies in states with more-severe and long-term economic shifts are receiving applicants seeking to move from manufacturing to service positions (Goeller, 2009). In Raleigh, North Carolina, applications for police positions more than doubled after the 2008 recession hit, despite the pessimism of command staff that the department's true staffing need might still never be met (S. Chambers, 2009). New York City has seen a flood of applicants to its shrinking department, including those from investment banking, an apparently new source of recruits (Schmidt, 2009).

Police leaders, however, question the long-term commitment of these candidates to their organization, particularly as jobs become more plentiful in other sectors (DeLord, 2009). Concerns about applicants' motivations, which arose in the burst of recruiting following the September 11, 2001, terrorist attacks, have matured into a crisis of confidence among recruiters and command staff about the quality of recruits (Domash, 2002; S. Chambers, 2009). Hiring standards remain the same for inexperienced candidates in areas where the economy has led to increases in applicants (Madrid, 2009). Having more applicants to screen increases the cost and substantive difficulty of assessing and selecting the best candidates for the job. More applications do not necessarily mean more qualified applicants; as one police executive warned, "You can't just hire anybody" (Codispoti, 2009).

At the same time, a weakened economy can also exacerbate staffing problems. Assuming a steady demand for police work, resource shortfalls that lead to furloughs, layoffs, and hiring freezes will expand both the staffing deficit and the true unmet demand for police service (Figure 2.1). Economic problems also highlight the uncertainty of the environments in which police departments must operate. Violent- and property-crime levels decreased during the recessionary year of 2008 (FBI, 2009). Such a decrease can be attributed partly to policing strategies that must continue in order to stave off potential increases but that constricting resources will make difficult to maintain (Camper and Brown, 2008; Moore, 2009).

Police staffing cuts resulting from the recession have occurred in jurisdictions ranging in size, geography, and organization from Santa Rosa, California (McCoy, 2009), to Gwinnett County, Georgia (Fox, 2009), to Toledo, Ohio (Rice, 2009), to Cook County, Illinois, to Sacramento, California (Johnson, 2008). Indeed, a 2008 survey by PERF (C. Fischer, 2009) revealed that 63 percent of responding agencies were preparing plans for funding cuts, with 31 percent of the cuts aimed at funding for sworn personnel, even after many of the agencies already made cuts to staffing via overtime reductions (62 percent), sworn-officer and civilian hiring freezes (27 and 53 percent, respectively), diminished recruit classes (34 percent), reducing employment levels through attrition (24 percent), furloughs (10 percent), and layoffs or forced retirements (7 percent).[1] Budget deficits are also causing cuts among police programs. For example, in addition to 132 sworn-deputy layoffs (after just saving 70 positions), the Sacramento Sheriff's Department grounded its helicopters, cut problem-oriented police units, and returned special weapons and tactics (SWAT) and canine officers to patrol to manage cuts to the department (R. Lewis, 2009). San Francisco police are skeptical that they can afford to fill existing foot-patrol positions, much less add recommended new ones (Sward, 2008). More broadly, the PERF (C. Fischer, 2009) survey indicated that 29 percent of responding agencies anticipated discontinuing special units (e.g., street crimes, narcotics, and community policing units). Such service cuts could intensify the workload of remaining police and increase the true level of unmet demand for police service.

---

[1] The sampling frame for and response rate of this survey is not evident in the report, so the generalizability of these findings is unclear.

While the economy has made it more difficult for police organizations to meet their workforce needs, the long-term systemic changes highlighted in this chapter suggest that staffing challenges will remain an issue even after the economy improves. Past hiring booms and freezes will create difficulties as they ripple through the organization over time—from field training and promotion to personnel budget consumption and retention. Resulting uneven distributions in the workforce can cause significant administrative challenges even in organizations that are fully staffed.

Conclusion

Police agencies face a threefold challenge in meeting the demand for officers: Attrition is increasing, sources of new recruits might be decreasing, and the demand for their work is expanding.

Attrition might increase as a result of the following:

- baby-boom generation retirements. In some agencies, large proportions of officers are near or eligible for retirement and could lead to a sharp decrease in staffing levels.
- military call-ups. A substantial number of agencies have officers who serve in military reserve forces; their deployment not only drains staff but also poses fiscal challenges through maintenance of benefits for them.
- changing generational expectations. Younger workers might have less organizational commitment than older ones and seek to change jobs more often in "boundary-less" careers.
- budget crises. Decreasing financial support to cover officer salaries limits some agencies' ability to prevent their officers from going to other agencies or even leaving the field.
- organizational characteristics. Immediate supervisors, career growth opportunities, recognition, and feedback can all affect whether an officer will stay or leave.

There are several causes as well to diminishing sources of new officers. Some of these are similar to those contributing to attrition. They include the following:

- a decrease in the qualified applicant pool. Large numbers of youths have used drugs, are out of shape, or have excessive debt.
- changing generational preferences. Similar to those that might get younger workers to leave the profession, changing generational preferences might lead younger workers to seek nonmilitaristic or more-flexible work.
- increased competition. The military, federal and state police agencies, private security firms, and other first-responder agencies recruit similar individuals, and competition for them has grown in the past decade.
- expanded skill requirements. Police work increasingly requires a broad range of skills that not all candidates might have.
- uncompetitive benefits. Police salaries lag those for many professions, although benefits and compensation for public employees have increased faster than those for private ones in the past decade.
- organizational characteristics. The image of a law-enforcement agency and the opportunities it offers, as well as the length and complexity of its hiring process, can all affect how many recruits might be attracted.

The potential for increased attrition and reduced supply makes it increasingly difficulty for police agencies to meet the expanding demand for their services. There are three principal causes of this expanding demand:

- community policing. The adoption of community policing has increased the number of functions local agencies must undertake, functions that require time and resources in addition to those for traditional police responsibilities.
- homeland security. In the past decade, local police have been asked to perform additional patrol and surveillance, gather and

analyze counterterrorism intelligence, conduct risk and threat assessments, and participate in many interagency task forces.
- emerging crimes. As a result of globalization, technological advancement, and greater awareness, the scope of crime that local agencies must address has expanded to include emerging crimes, such as human trafficking, identity theft, and cybercrime.

Further complicating these issues, especially recruitment and retention efforts, has been a weakened economy of recent years, reducing or restricting the options available to local agencies. In the next two chapters, we discuss in more depth what local agencies can do to retain and recruit officers. Because retention can reduce the need for recruitment, we focus on it first.

CHAPTER THREE

Retention: Plugging the Hole in the Bucket

"Our people are our most important asset" is a frequently used phrase in police management. This saying magnifies why employee turnover is an important issue facing police organizations. Crucial issues related to employee turnover include its consequences for an organization, what it indicates about organizational health and functioning (e.g., the efficiency of personnel management and planning), and the changing nature of modern-day policing. In this chapter, we place issues of police turnover in context by examining what is known about retaining officers, as well as experiences from other fields that might support different approaches to officer retention.

What Is Turnover?

Turnover occurs when an employee leaves an organization. It is costly and challenges organizational stability (Mueller and Price, 1989). There are two major types of turnover, each with its own effects (Edwards, 2007; T. Lee and Mitchell, 1994; Hom and Griffeth, 1994). Understanding each can help provide an approach to targeting the problem and reducing its costs (Kacmar et al., 2006). The first type of turnover is *involuntary turnover*, occurring when an employer terminates the working relationship with an employee (i.e., the employee is not leaving voluntarily). The second is *voluntary turnover*, occurring when an employee chooses to leave an organization. Other labels for involuntary turnover include *planned*, *desired*, *functional*, and *unavoidable turnover*; those for voluntary turnover include *unplanned*, *undesired*, *dysfunctional*, and *avoidable turnover* (Edwards, 2007).

Within these two broad types of turnover, there are many variations. For example, terminations, while a form of involuntary turnover, are not unavoidable (Ahlrichs, 2000). Terminations generally reflect bad hiring or bad management; both are avoidable and critical to improve. Such distinctions and measures for them can help identify the best ways to address retention problems. Yet, most agencies that measure turnover combine voluntary and involuntary turnover in one measure—that is, they assess total employee separation as a proportion of total employees in the organization. Alternatively, organizations might assess avoidable turnover as total employee separations less unavoidable turnover as a proportion of total employees. Organizations might also assess turnover by length of service; position in the organization, zone, or district; age; race; ethnicity; gender; and cohort. Table 3.1 offers several ratios that can be used alone or in combination to understand organizational turnover.

Effects of Turnover

Turnover has both positive and negative effects on an organization and its employees. Allowing agencies to rid themselves of poor performers is often good and helps the organization advance, introduce new ideas, increase productivity and performance, and facilitate change (Ahlrichs, 2000; Birati and Tziner, 1995; Hom and Griffeth, 1994; McEvoy and Cascio, 1987; Williams and Livingstone, 1994). Even some transfer of good employees elsewhere can help an organization; if a transferred employee performs well in a new position, then the original employer's reputation is enhanced (Orrick, 2008a). Employee transfers might also enhance contacts and networks in both agencies. At the same time, the loss of experienced personnel can adversely affect an organization in both reputation and costs. Tsang and Zahra (2008, p. 1441) call this "organizational forgetting," resulting in the "deterioration of an organization's knowledge base."

Curiously, law-enforcement agencies rarely examine the costs of turnover, perhaps because turnover costs are rarely identified by a line item in a department's budget. Even those departments estimating costs

Table 3.1
Summary of Example Employee Turnover Ratios

Type of Turnover	Formula
Overall	Number of separations ÷ number of employees
Avoidable	(Number of separations – unavoidable separations) ÷ number of employees
Involuntary	(Number of separations – voluntary separations) ÷ number of employees
Recent hire	Number of separations of employees with <2 years of experience ÷ number of employees with <2 years of experience
Cohort	Number of new hires this month ÷ number of new hires still on the job in 6 months

tend to focus on the short-term costs of replacing an officer and ignore organizational investments that have compounded over the years. Orrick (2002, 2008a) describes the comprehensive costs of police turnover, suggesting a wide-ranging set of costs beyond the obvious recruitment costs, as summarized in Table 3.2.

Police employee success is a function of officer experience and ability to make sensible decisions with little supervision or oversight (Frost, 2006; Gottfredson and Gottfredson, 1988). By reducing the number of officers with experience, turnover inhibits effective decisionmaking. It diminishes the strength and cohesion a department gains by having experienced staff, and that cannot be replaced over time. Agencies with higher turnover and less experienced officers suffer reduced productivity and more-frequent complaints (Orrick, 2002). The cost of training sworn police officers is substantial, particularly in comparison to other fields (New South Wales Council on the Cost of Government, 1996). The high level of organizational and job-specific knowledge required of police officers also means that high turnover can impair organizational performance and service delivery while replacement personnel are selected and trained.

Other fields experience similar problems. These include "brain drain" following voluntary separations that reduce performance levels and increase operational risks (Birati and Tziner, 1995; Mobley, 1982;

Table 3.2
Summary of Costs Associated with Police Turnover

Cost Category	Cost Example
Recruitment	Advertising Recruiters' salaries Bonuses
Selection	Tests Review-board salaries Investigator salaries Medical, psychological, and drug screening
New employee	Payroll and computer personnel New uniforms and equipment
Training	Orientation and field training Recruit salaries and benefits Field-trainer salaries Supervision In-service training
Operating	Overtime to cover vacancies Loss of productivity as employee departs Increased further turnover Peer disruption Disruption or loss of community relationships Disruption of department operations Lower morale Missed deadlines Increased further turnover
Intangible	Loss of knowledge and experience Peer disruption Disruption or loss of community relationships Disruption of department operations Lower morale Missed deadlines

Holtom, Mitchell, Lee, and Eberly, 2008). While these costs are difficult to quantify, they are just as real as salaries and training costs. Economic conditions can make them more pronounced: The offer of early retirement coupled with an inability to hire new officers, both resulting from fiscal difficulties, promises to accelerate the "brain drain" (Faher, 2009; Womack, 2009).

One effort to quantify the costs of turnover suggests that replacing an officer with three years experience costs more than twice his or her annual salary (Orrick, 2002). These costs can substantially differ by levels of training provided to an officer, salary and benefits paid, and selection procedures for new officers. At one extreme, in 2003, it cost approximately $100,000 for Los Angeles and $250,000 for the federal government to train new law-enforcement officers (Frost, 2006). More typically, in 2009, it cost approximately $58,000 to select, hire, and train a new officer, a still substantial expense whose magnitude is attributable in part to selection and training processes that are unique to policing (Copeland, 2009). In contrast to those in many other fields, police selection procedures include background investigations, medical examinations, interviews, psychological assessments, drug screening, physical agility tests, and department-specific training.

Agencies might be able to improve retention by experimenting with strategies from other fields (Tadwalkar and Sen, 2005). Reducing turnover can help mitigate recruiting difficulties resulting from a smaller pool of qualified applicants or shifting generational preferences (Hom and Griffeth, 1994; Copeland, 2009).

Is Turnover a Particularly Difficult Problem for Law Enforcement?

While turnover can pose many problems for police agencies, its extent, particularly in comparison to that in other professions, is unclear. Several studies have identified attrition of officers as a major problem facing police departments (Frost, 2006; Harris and Baldwin, 1999; NIJ, 1992; Webster and Connors, 1988; Gettinger, 1984). Yet, despite the significant and well-placed concern about police turnover, other research indicates that turnover in police agencies is lower than in other sectors. Annual voluntary turnover rates are regarded as excessive when they surpass the 10-percent mark in law-enforcement or correctional agencies (Doerner, 1995). These are lower than the rates for teachers, at 17 percent (Planty et al., 2008). Overall turnover rates for state and local government positions, including police and sheriffs' patrol officers, are only about a third of that for all (nonfarm) jobs (BLS, undated).

A British study of turnover in police agencies found an increasing number of resignations and transfers but a comparatively low turnover rate of 6 percent for policing as a whole (Christine Cooper and Ingram, 2004). Average labor turnover across all sectors was 18 percent in 2000 and 2001; staff turnover was 15 percent in central government and 16 percent in local government. Analysis of data from Australian and New Zealand police jurisdictions also found a low level of turnover from 1999 to 2003. Benchmarking data showed that total turnover of sworn officers was lower in Australasian police organizations than for employees in Australian public-sector organizations and comparable to turnover of employees in international public-sector organizations (Lynch and Tuckey, 2004).

U.S. research shows similarly low turnover rates in a variety of police agencies. A study of police turnover in Vermont found an average statewide turnover rate of 6 percent between 2001 and 2006 (Litcher, Reister, and Mason, 2006). A 2004 study of North Carolina found that attrition ranged from 0 to 87 percent, with an average of 14 percent (Yearwood and Freeman, 2004). In Prince William County, Virginia, the turnover rate in 2004 was 13 percent—double the 2003 rate (Kearns, 2007). Turnover rates in Chesterfield County, Virginia, have fluctuated between 4 and 6 percent in recent years (Edwards, 2007). Orrick (2008a) found that the average turnover ranged from 5 to 21 percent. A 2001 survey reports that 72 percent of respondents indicate that retention constitutes a crucial policing problem, with 54 percent reporting that the problem had grown (L. Lee, 2001).

Although turnover rates appear lower in police agencies than in many other sectors, police-officer turnover can carry greater costs than turnover elsewhere because of the expense of selecting and training officers.

Police turnover is higher and more challenging for small municipal departments than for county or state agencies (McIntyre, 1990). A 1999 study found turnover in smaller departments (i.e., those serving fewer than 50,000 persons) to be 7 percent, compared to 5 percent in larger agencies (Koper, Maguire, and Moore, 2001). Similarly, smaller agencies in North Carolina reportedly had an attrition rate (18 percent) twice that of their larger counterparts (Yearwood, 2003).

Officers in smaller agencies also have differing career paths from those in larger ones. For example, two-thirds of officers departing smaller agencies do so with less than five years of service, compared to just one-third of those at larger ones (Hoffman, 1993).

Who Leaves, and When Do They Go?

Recent research distinguishes among those who exit the profession. In particular, it suggests that young persons and new officers, as well as women and minorities, leave policing in disproportionate numbers.

K. Riley, Turner, et al. (2005) found that more than one-third of officers who left the Cincinnati force had less than one year of service and that nearly two-thirds who left had less than five years. Haarr (2005), using a panel survey of 446 recruits entering Arizona police academies, found that 13 percent dropped out before completing the academy and an additional 22 percent dropped out during field training or before completing their first year on a force. Nearly all the separations in Cincinnati and Arizona were voluntary. Yearwood and Freeman (2004) found an average length of stay of 34 months in North Carolina police departments. Lynch and Tuckey (2008) also found that young officers (i.e., those no more than 31 years of age) were more likely to leave policing than those in later stages of their career. They also found some difference between men and women in attrition, although length of service could also affect this relationship. There is also some churn among early career officers. While the California Commission on Peace Officer Standards and Training (Switzer, 2006) found that more than three in four officers work for only one agency in their career, it also found that, among those who transfer, 25 percent do so within 1.3 years and 50 percent do so within 3.2 years. After the first year, the average annual number of officers who leave is fairly stable (about 2 percent).

Lynch and Tuckey (2004) found that women most likely to leave New Zealand police forces were between 25 and 39 years of age. A longitudinal study of 125 recruits in Britain also found female officers more likely to resign than males, and younger recruits more likely to resign than older ones (Fielding and Fielding, 1987). Though most research finds gender differences in police retention, there are some exceptions. Haarr (2005) found that, although the number of women entering police work is small, there was no statistically significant difference between males and females in the rate of dropout from police work.

Regarding race and ethnicity, Doerner (1995) found that 48 percent of white officers and 51 percent of black officers hired in a five-year study period (1981–1986) left the Tallahassee Police Department and that black officers were more likely than white officers to depart involuntarily during their field-training phase. Haarr (2005) found statistically significant differences in rates of dropout *among* racial and ethnic minorities, with Latino and Native American officers having significantly higher dropout rates than African American recruits.

Officers leaving later in their careers might do so for reasons that accumulate over time, as Christine Cooper and Ingram (2004) found in a study of ten British agencies. Buzawa (1979) found a nonlinear relationship between experience and job satisfaction in the Detroit and Oakland (Calif.) police departments. Buzawa, Austin, and Bannon (1994), in addition to confirming this relationship, found patrol officers more dissatisfied than others with their jobs, particularly regarding supervision and advancement and promotional opportunities, and some decrease in satisfaction over time. Police agencies, if facing a wave of retirements, might seek to retain officers through a variety of policies, including deferred-retirement-option programs offering some tax breaks (Orrick, 2008a). Yet, as Tadwalker and Sen (2005) write, retention and turnover programs should be more than targeted prevention strategies. Properly designed, they can address early- and midcareer reasons officers leave and reduce turnover at all stages of a career.

Why Do Officers Leave?

T. Lee and Mitchell (1994, p. 31) portray voluntary turnover as a "complex process whereby individuals assess their feelings, personal situation, and work environment, and over time, make decisions about staying or leaving an organization." Similarly, Christine Cooper and Ingram (2004) found that officer decisions to leave often took place over a considerable period of time and did not result from one decisive event. Curiously, nearly half of those who left indicated that they would consider returning to the force, giving further credence to the contention that the turnover decision is a complex psychological process—and possibly pointing to ways police agencies could improve retention.

No overarching theory on why officers leave is evident in existing research, but the five main influences Lynch and Tuckey (2004) identify as influencing turnover point to a tentative model (Figure 3.1). The five main influences are (1) the pull of other opportunities; (2) actual and potential compensation; (3) personal characteristics and demographic factors; (4) organizational health, policy, and culture; and (5) employee needs. All contribute, albeit unequally, to turnover. By our tentative model, these influences all determine job satisfaction and organizational commitment (or lack thereof), which, in turn, might lead to exit. Research generally supports job satisfaction and organizational commitment as critical antecedents to turnover (Hom and Griffeth, 1994; Tett and Meyer, 2006). In the next sections, we review each of these influences and how agencies might address them.

Other Opportunities

Orrick (2008a) has pointed to economic factors as strong external forces that influence the turnover decision. Officers might leave for perceived better economic opportunities. Opportunities from outside the

Figure 3.1
Conceptual Model of Determinants of Attrition

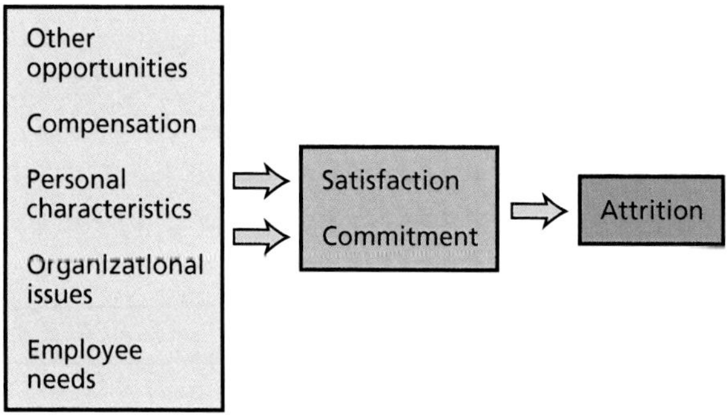

RAND *MG959-3.1*

profession might push an officer from it; better opportunities in the profession might pull officers to them in a form of "cannibalism" within the field (DeLord, 2009). To counter other opportunities, Orrick (2008a) suggests that departments maintain conditions to minimize the "push" from outside the profession and to enhance the "pull" of their own agency. The economic recession of 2008 and 2009 might stabilize how other opportunities push officers from the field or pull them elsewhere within it. Nevertheless, the impact of external economic trends merit further research to determine their full effect on turnover.

Compensation

Compensation includes not only salary and benefits but also viable career ladders, adequate training and equipment, and perceptions by officers that a policing career will afford a good life. To be sure, managers view salary and benefits as the biggest element of compensation affecting turnover. Yearwood and Freeman (2004) found that nearly half of North Carolina agencies attribute at least 70 percent of their attrition to compensation issues driving officers to other departments or professions. Furthermore, as Branham (2005) notes, inadequate compensation can contribute to feelings of devaluation that grow into more-potent reasons for leaving.

Inadequate compensation also enhances the influence of other factors on turnover, such as promotional opportunities and procedural justice (Rostker, Hix, and Wilson, 2007). Indeed, a study of 20,000 workers from 18 industries found that between 80 and 90 percent of employees decide to leave an organization for reasons other than money (C. Lee, 2006). Such reasons include their job, their manager, and the culture and environment of their work. As Christopher Lee (2006, p. 53) notes,

> pay is usually a symptom of other things not going well. When employees complain about pay, they are usually indirectly indicating that they are not happy with their work situation. Pay is a lightning rod issue as it is more tangible than poor management and lack of appreciation.

Although the issue of compensation is paramount to understanding sources of employee turnover, it can distract from other substantive and more deeply embedded issues, such as organizational culture, leadership, and employee engagement.

Why might managers perceive compensation to be the cause of turnover more than is actually the case? Orrick (2008a) notes several possible reasons.[1] First, officers might cite pay as the reason for leaving to keep good relations with their department. Second, using compensation as an absolute for leaving appears simple for the officer who wants to leave, making the process quick and free of additional trauma. Third, attributing attrition to compensation allows management to avoid addressing other problems or conflicts.

As long as employees view compensation as fair in comparison to others in the same organization and to others in the field, it will not be the most significant contributor to turnover. To enhance salary fairness, police agencies must modernize their pay and benefit structures (Orrick, 2008a). Addressing perceived fairness can be difficult in times of economic stress and resulting wage freezes and furloughs ("Even Cops Losing Their Jobs in Recession," 2009; Sward, 2008).

Officers might also seek fairness in promotions and career growth, issues directly intertwined with salary and affecting employee engagement. Rostker, Hix, and Wilson (2007) note that the New Orleans Police Department's infrequent promotion opportunities and inability to give pay increases hindered officer motivation and retention. Orrick (2008a) claims that career opportunities might be more important to younger generations of employees who seek immediate gratification. Buzawa, Austin, and Bannon (1994) also suggest that lack of promotional opportunity leads to increased job dissatisfaction over time. In small agencies, there is not much room for specialization, and recruits must wait their turn for higher-level assignments; in larger agencies, there is greater task specialization, which can lead to boredom and feelings of being trapped by skill sets (Orrick, 2008a; Haarr, 2005). This problem can affect even new recruits. As Haarr (2005) notes, new recruits might think that the job they were hired to do is exciting but, once on the job, find that many of its daily duties are mundane. Job scheduling might contribute to these realizations. Some might also expect more flexibility

[1] The work of Orrick, the public safety director for the city of Cordele, Georgia, is useful for being among the few to address these issues—hence our heavy reliance on it in several places in this monograph. Nevertheless, we caution the reader that some of his insights are based on experience or anecdotes rather than systematic research.

allowing for work-family balance and self-initiated work partnerships, as well as quicker advancement opportunities.

Differences between expectations and realities can quickly lead to turnover if not addressed early. Upon entering the force, those ultimately resigning and those staying did not differ in their attitudes regarding job pay, status, or security, but, by the end of the first year, resigners reported greater dissatisfaction with these and less commitment to police work (Fielding and Fielding, 1987). Resigners also expressed greater dissatisfaction with the amount of paperwork, social isolation, and the public image of the job.

Officers without proper training can also become discouraged. Employees today expect frequent training opportunities to improve their abilities. Without such training, they can lose confidence (Orrick, 2008a). Many officers now also consider equipment to be part of their "compensation"; the chief of the Pittsburgh Bureau of Police in particular has noted that, given limits on recruiting resources, providing updated equipment to officers can help attract and retain them (J. Wilson and Grammich, 2009a). Officers often cite frustration about not having adequate or functional equipment to perform their jobs. This too can lead to turnover (Orrick, 2008a).

Personal Characteristics

Personal characteristics, such as education and personality traits, can also affect turnover (Christine Cooper and Ingram, 2004), although how is sometimes unclear. Research on the effects of education, for example, is inconsistent—showing, in different cases, a positive, negative, or no relationship with job satisfaction (Dantzker, 1994; Frost, 2006; Lynch and Tuckey, 2004). Griffin, Dunbar, and McGill (1978) found that all police officers surveyed in a southwestern police department were satisfied with their jobs regardless of their education level and that job satisfaction remained constant across educational levels. Subsequent research has found that the relationship between educational attainment and job satisfaction varies by department (Buzawa, 1984; Dantzker, 1993).

Regarding personality traits, Drew, Carless, and Thompson (2008) found that those with high anxiety are more likely to exit, while those who are tough-minded and venturesome are less likely to do so. They found no relationship between turnover and one's openness to experience. Nor did they find a relationship between turnover and one's agreeableness. Such findings could help in developing a typology of police turnover, fusing explanatory theories from diverse fields and using policing as the potential landscape of evaluating turnover conditions (Hom and Griffeth, 1994).

Organizational Issues

Organizational health, policy, and culture are powerful predictors of employee turnover. These issues include organizational function, generational competence, supervision and leadership, bureaucracy, fairness, and openness and transparency.

There is considerable evidence that organizational dysfunction increases turnover. Orrick (2008a) suggests that many law-enforcement agencies are characterized by "silo management styles"—that is, they are tall, rank-heavy, and hierarchical organizational structures requiring compliance with policies, procedures, rules, and regulation enforcement. Fry and Berkes (1983) trace the influence of this management style on policing from the industrial age and its requirements for rigid organization. Such a structure can hinder growth (Auten, 1981; Fry and Berkes, 1983) and produce frustrations that increase turnover, especially among younger officers (Orrick, 2008a). Edwards (2007) suggests that younger generations lack the ability to succeed in the "silo," the paramilitary organizational environment endemic to many police agencies. Others suggest that such a structure prevents police organizations from fulfilling career needs of younger generations (Brand, 1999; M. Fischer, 2006; McCafferty, 2003).

Employees might also leave organizations because of poor supervision and leadership (Christine Cooper and Ingram, 2004; Lynch and Tuckey, 2004; Orrick, 2008a, 2008b). The relationship that immediate and midlevel supervisors have with their employees often has the most influence on an officer's decision to stay or leave a department. As Orrick (2008b) said, "people don't quit jobs, they quit bosses." Among supervisor behaviors that Orrick (2008a) suggests contribute to officer attrition are setting poor examples, indecisiveness, unfairness, being overly critical or not sharing credit for work, and poor communication. Loss of trust and confidence in senior leaders also adversely affects retention, especially to the extent that leaders embrace traditional management models and fail to communicate their vision to employees. This indicates the importance of training supervisors to mentor employees, and determining whether police bureaucracy might discourage good candidates from applying for supervisory positions (COPS, 2009b).

Policies and procedures can also affect a police officer's attitudes, behaviors, and feelings toward organization and self (Frost, 2006; Kappeler, Sluder, and Alpert, 1994; Patterson, 1992; Violanti and Aron, 1995). Some researchers suggest that employees will be more satisfied with decisions if they perceive the processes used for making them to be fair (Frost, 2006; Thibaut and Walker, 1975). Procedural justice has been linked to organizational commitment (Folger and Konovsky, 1989), job satisfaction, loyalty, and employee evaluation of supervisor and organization (Frost, 2006). Given the importance of organizational fairness to job satisfaction, organizational commitment, and retention, law-enforcement agencies can create a satisfied and committed workforce with minimal cost through the use of procedurally fair policies. This is especially true for younger recruits, who have a heightened perception of organizational fairness and distributive justice (Brand, 1999; Frost, 2006).

Organizational openness and transparency are also critical to procedural fairness. Employees who are invited to participate in decisionmaking are more likely to find the process fair (Cohen-Charash and Spector, 2001). Officers of today will become less satisfied and committed to organizations that are less open and transparent and do not allow for input and feedback (Lambert, 2003).

Employee Needs

Employee needs include feedback and recognition, a stimulating work environment, job satisfaction, organizational commitment, and connectedness. A thorough understanding of employee needs can help organizations understand why some employees leave, particularly when a sound reason is not evident.

Orrick (2008a) suggests that recruits today have more higher-order needs of belongingness, love, self-esteem, and self-actualization. As curious and nebulous as such needs might seem to police management, departments must meet them if they expect to retain younger officers. Orrick further suggests that employee turnover is an emotional issue and that workers quit because they feel that their need for trust, hope, worth, or competence is not being met. Other researchers concur that meeting these needs might be more salient for younger generations of workers than for previous generations (Brand, 1999; M. Fischer, 2006; McCafferty, 2003).

Similarly, employees want to know how they are performing, and providing frequent feedback is crucial to a contented and high-performing workforce (Orrick, 2008a). Lack of feedback can also lead to serious mistakes, which can degrade confidence, morale, and job satisfaction. Positive reinforcement or recognition can improve performance and increase job satisfaction and organizational commitment. Unfortunately, good performance often goes unrewarded, while considerable time and energy is spent critiquing poor performance.

Building on the concept of job satisfaction, Reiser (1974) proposed a theoretical link between police turnover and burnout caused by job stress accumulating over time. In a study of Memphis police officers who voluntarily resigned from police work between 1975 and 1980, Sparger and Giacopassi (1983) concluded that veteran officers voluntarily resigned because of "burnout" resulting from the culmination of occupational frustrations and dissatisfactions related to traditional authoritarian management styles, organizational policies, departmental politics, lack of appreciation for their efforts, the system of internal discipline, pay and fringe benefits, relations with civic officials, court policies, and community expectations. They also cited the influence of intense on-the-job situations, a lack of self-fulfillment in higher-order needs, family considerations, and the conduct of co-workers. More recently, Dick (2000) analyzed clinical data from therapy with police officers who were under stress and considering leaving the police force and cited "epiphenal events" as causing emotional exhaustion and burnout. Such events lead officers to conclude that the organization stands in the way of their ability to make their desired, positive contribution through work.

Other research suggests that employees leave after realizing they are no longer committed to the organization or the career path. Diminishing job satisfaction leads workers to question their commitment to the organization or their career, which precipitates the decision to leave it (Frost, 2006; Lambert and Hogan, 2009; Jaramillo, Nixon, and Sams, 2005). Job satisfaction plays a crucial role in retention, often extending the concept to include job embeddedness, including, as Mitchell, Holtom, Lee, Sablynski, and Erez (2001) suggest, formal and informal connections with other persons on and off the job (including co-workers, community members, and family), an element of fit (that is, employee perceptions of compatibility with the work environment), and sacrifice (the perceived loss of material or psychological benefits that might be forfeited by leaving a job). Workers who are embedded in their jobs are less likely to leave than those who are not.

What Can Agencies Do to Prevent Turnover?

Unfortunately, the research on what agencies can do to reduce turnover appears to rely more on anecdotal accounts than on empirical analysis. Nevertheless, in this section, we highlight existing knowledge about several strategies, citing evidence where it exists, but cautioning that each strategy should be considered critically, given the lack of rigorous analyses. These strategies can be generally be classified in one of five categories (see Table 3.3): (1) planning and analysis, (2) reducing the financial impact of turnover, (3) enhancing compensation and perks, (4) employee engagement strategies, and (5) improving organizational effectiveness. Many practices cross these categories.

Planning and Analysis

Conduct an Evidence-Based Analysis of Department Retention Needs. While there is some federal government data collection and analysis for police personnel planning (Wilson, 2006), the law-enforcement community can also draw on data compiled and analyses conducted for other professions to gauge applicability to its own work. For example, the U.S. military has conducted national studies on generational preferences, attitudes, perceptions, and broad demographic change over time in

Table 3.3
Means of Limiting the Effects of Turnover

Strategy Category	Strategy
Plan and analyze	Conduct evidence-based analysis of retention needs. Know employees and their needs. Advocate for staff. Conduct exit and "stay" interviews.
Reduce financial impact	Use realistic job previews. Consider assessment-center methods in hiring and promoting. Hire pretrained or precertified employees. Think twice about service contracts.
Enhance compensation and perks	Define "compensation" broadly. Pay employees what they are worth. Offer apprentice salary during training. Offer education incentives. Create an incentive "portfolio." Use career ladders. Consider offering perks—but wisely. Investigate job flexibility.
Engage employees	Understand what engagement is and how to do it. Allow employees to experience others' duties through work diversity. Provide job shadowing. Give employees a voice in decisionmaking. Allow for meaningful employee feedback. Recognize employee success. Mentor beyond field training.
Improve organizational effectiveness	Communicate goals routinely and effectively. Be fair and transparent in all aspects of policy. Reduce unnecessary bureaucracy. Select and maintain effective leaders.

order to identify changing career preferences in the armed services. Such data can also yield insights on changes that will affect law enforcement (Miller, 2008). For example, agencies can incorporate local demographic and market trends, as well as project the retirement-eligible portion and potential attrition rates of their workforces, to develop retention and succession plans and task forces. Such task forces have existed at least since the early 2000s, including in four California departments (L. Lee, 2001). As agencies traditionally conduct needs assessments to determine which changes are appropriate for their specific needs, they can apply evidence-based analyses of needs to map approaches for reducing turnover.

Know Your Employees and Their Needs. Organizations can develop a dynamic understanding of their workforces by conducting regular surveys about employee job satisfaction and organizational commitment. These results might assist in improving not only short-term retention but also long-term job and organizational commitment. These surveys should attempt to differentiate among groups, including women, minorities, ranks, generations, new employees, and near-retirees. Knowing employees and their individual needs intimately is a hallmark of a proactive human-resource department and can lead to targeted problem-solving when retention becomes a problem (Haggerty, 2009). Following other accountability models commonplace in modern policing (e.g., CompStat in New York City), agencies should consider holding individual supervisors and managers accountable for retaining their staff, establishing stronger at-stake relationships between supervisor and line officer (Lim et al., 2009; J. Wilson and Grammich, 2009a).

Go Beyond "Knowing" to Advocating for Your Staff. Even though human capital is the most important and expensive asset for police agencies, few agencies have devoted resources to understanding it. The best place to start understanding it is within the organization, where direct supervisors can communicate with upper management about potential problems. It is important to identify at-risk employees, lest hidden problems lead to turnover (Haggerty, 2009; Orrick, 2008a). Officers might tell other officers or their supervisors that they are looking to leave the organization, and they might contemplate leaving for some time (Christine Cooper and Ingram, 2004). Key transitions leading to attrition can include the birth of a child, children graduating from high school or college, divorce, and separation of a close friend from the department. Knowing of such events can perhaps help departments assist officers in times of personal transition. Agencies should communicate with officers exhibiting prolonged frustration or disappointment after being passed over for promotion and explain why the promotion cycle might have been unsuccessful for them, making the experience a foundation for future success. Officers requesting much time off might also be indicating risk for turnover that their department can address (Haggerty,

2009). Officers might request meetings with human resources to view their record or to discuss retirement options, but real outreach efforts by immediate supervisors to establish support systems for officers can provide valuable opportunities to promote retention.

Conduct Exit and "Stay" Interviews, Integrating the Results into Long-Term Planning. Exit interviews can yield information on turnover. Lynch and Tuckey (2004) recommend that these interviews be conducted by an independent person away from the work site and that the data be kept anonymously and separately from individual employee records. Exit interviews can also be used to educate employees about how they can come back to the agency. Stay interviews, or interviews with current employees aimed at exploring the reasons they stay with the organization, can be a more proactive approach to achieving the same goal of improving retention (Herman, 2005). These approaches can help agencies understand the reasons for turnover, retain good relationships with former employees, and signal current employees that their retention is important. Despite the information they can offer, few agencies undertake exit interviews (Taylor et al., 2006). Furthermore, less than 30 percent of California departments use employee input to address retention, and only 15 percent have a written plan to improve officer retention (L. Lee, 2001). Planning and analysis with the guidance of a human-resource specialist can yield data and information to address turnover problems.

Reducing the Financial Impact of Turnover

Use Realistic Job Previews for Interested Applicants Up Front. A realistic job preview includes a number of strategies to cut through impressionistic and unrealistic expectations of careers and give glimpses into the true nature of the work performed. For example, the Idaho State Police attempts to demystify the policing career by providing, on its recruitment website, examples of daily duties and responsibilities expected of its troopers (Idaho State Police, undated). The International Association of Chiefs of Police's "Discover Policing" website features realistic vignettes, interviews, and commentary to provide interested applicants with not-so-glamorous views of real police work (IACP, undated). These could be incorporated into department recruitment strategies along with job announcements and observation opportunities (such as ride-alongs and job shadowing) that accurately depict the work. Round-table discussions could also improve recruits' sense of career paths. Candid videos describing progression from the academy to the beat to detective work to leadership positions might also be useful. Such techniques might be appropriate not only for attracting new hires but also for retaining officers.

Unrealistic expectations might result in internal (recruitment) or external (media reports) difficulties. Realistic job previews can help not only adjust expectations but also save departments money. Companies that use these strategies saved an average of approximately $711 per employee (Kickul, 2002; Phillips, 1998)—savings that would likely be higher in policing, given the costs of finding and training new officers. This approach to providing realistic job expectations also has morale benefits. Employees who feel misled about job expectations might compensate by withholding work or commitment to the organization (Kickul, 2002; Meglino, Ravlin, and DeNisi, 2000). Such sense of betrayal can also fuel further turnover (Becker and Dale, 2003; Pitt and Ramaseshan, 1995).

Consider Assessment-Center Methods in Hiring and Promoting. After establishing an applicant pool, law-enforcement agencies go to great lengths to assess candidates for initial hiring or promotion. Many police departments use written entrance or promotional exams, as well as an assessment center. An assessment center is where a series of exercises is conducted in which each participant demonstrates skills to a group of observers, or assessors, who rate the candidates. The International Congress on Assessment Center Methods has established certain standards including an analysis of job specifications, classification of behaviors, multiple assessment approaches, and job-related simulations (Moses and Boehm, 1975). Substantial evidence suggests that using an assessment-center approach improves hiring practices, raises morale, and leads to an applicant pool with a more comprehensive view of job expectations (B. Chambers, 2002; LaHuis, 2005; Riggio, Mayes, and Schleicher, 2003). However, as we discuss in the next chapter, some contend that the career needs and goals of new generations of recruits might be incompatible with assessment-center methods (DeCicco, 2000; Orrick, 2008a; Taylor et al., 2006).

Hire Pretrained or Precertified Employees. Many police agencies hire candidates who have already completed some professional training or law-enforcement certification either with prior employers or at their own individual expense. The extent of such pretraining, and agencies' willingness to hire individuals with such training, varies widely (International Association of Directors of Law Enforcement Standards and Training, 2005). Agencies might realize a variety of benefits from recruiting pretrained officers. Recruits with prior military training tend to have lower attrition during agency training, higher retention, and higher training readiness (Golfin, 2006). Productivity might increase as agencies fill vacancies more rapidly with candidates who have acute knowledge and skills (Viney, Adamson, and Doherty, 1997). Shifting recruitment selection from organization to candidate can also strengthen personal job fit over time (N. Anderson and Cunningham-Snell, 2000). Such cities as Oakland, California, have begun recruiting pretrained candidates as part of their overall hiring strategy to bring the department to full staffing (Poulson, 2008). Pretrained officers might undergo abbreviated academy sessions in which initial basic training need not be offered, saving training costs for the department (Haggerty, 2009). Agencies might also use differential compensation to attract the best pretrained officers (Kowal, Hassel, and Hassel, 2008).

Although offering some financial benefits to departments, hiring pretrained candidates can also pose risks. Departments should not expect candidates to have dramatically improved performance when the quality of previous training is unknown (Viney, Adamson, and Doherty, 1997). They should also ensure that their own training is not redundant (Golfin, 2006) and focuses on agency-specific needs (R. Byrne, 2001). Hiring pretrained candidates who are attractive to other agencies can also escalate short-term turnover (R. Byrne, 2001). Many agencies have cultural fears of hiring pretrained candidates that can be overcome with an understanding of the risks and benefits of hiring such candidates (Golfin, 2006).

Think Twice About Service Contracts. Police departments might also require contracts of new hires so as to reduce direct costs of employee turnover (Orrick, 2008a). Under some service contracts, new hires leaving the agency within three years of initial employment must reimburse prorated training expenses to the agency. Agencies might also use such contracts when sending an employee to long-term or expensive training. Nevertheless, their use has not been shown to reduce turnover—only to lessen the financial risk associated with hiring new employees (Orrick, 2008a), though research in policing is limited. Mestemaker (1991) found little benefit of a career-based Air Force service requirement program on retention. A program service commitment in exchange for signing and retention bonuses, designed to retain health-care employees in nursing residency, met with mixed results, including a 50-percent retention rate after two years (Olson et al., 2001). Because these contracts might contradict worker expectations of flexibility, organizations should consider them carefully (Lawler, 2005; Perrons, 2000).

The use of loyalty contracts has decreased in part because of globalization and increasing workforce skills (Lawler, 2005) and the belief that written contracts cast doubts on informal, trusting relationships (often referred to as *psychological contracts* between employer and worker). Workers find such contracts unattractive because they can limit mobility and often diminish trust between management and employees (Flood et al., 2001; Lawler, 2005).

Enhancing Compensation and Other Benefits

Define "Compensation" Broadly. Although, as noted, research suggests that compensation often masks other reasons for leaving an organization, it and other benefits are powerful motivators for retention. Higher or well-timed salary adjustments, more-frequent promotions, visible career ladders, housing allowances, take-home cars, on-site child care, health-club memberships, and job flexibility are some of the benefits that can help improve retention. Officers might compare such benefits across agencies and might transfer to agencies with better benefit packages. Currently, most police departments follow a one-size-fits-all approach to compensating employees, meaning that all entering recruits, for example, are offered the same salary and benefit package; younger workers might reject this model and look for options that better suit their needs (Edwards, 2007). Lavigna (2005, p. 150) explains:

> Compensation must be used strategically to make the most difference. This means abandoning systems that rely on rigid across-the-board raises. Managers should be able to use their discretion (within guidelines) to hire above the minimum and give raises and bonuses for good performance and retention.

Fairness, rather than the level of compensation, is more important for retention (Edwards, 2007). Money itself is not enough to engage all generations of employees (Edwards, 2007). Commitment and loyalty, especially of younger workers, to an organization cannot be "bought" (Brand, 1999; M. Fischer, 2006; McCafferty, 2003). The challenge is to find nonmonetary ways to motivate and engage workers. Today, benefit flexibility or a cafeteria-style approach is an option many companies have tried, allowing options while keeping costs down (Edwards, 2007).

Pay Your Employees What They Are Worth. Increased compensation can also be effective, especially if it is well timed. The literature is sparse on this issue, but well-placed and well-timed longevity pay, most likely coupled with other benefits to meet individual needs, might reduce turnover. Longevity pay can boost retention of long-term, highly skilled and experienced personnel. Although there are direct costs to such pay, these likely outweigh the costs of turnover. These increases should be timed to the agency's key attrition points. A similar approach, called a *retention bonus*, is being used effectively within the Lehigh Valley Health Network. This program pays bonuses from $3,000 to $5,000 at specified times to reward employees who stay with the hospital (Edwards, 2007). These bonuses have led to low turnover rates and an abundance of applicants, landing the hospital on both *Fortune*'s 100 Best Companies to Work For and *U.S. News and World Report*'s Best Hospitals list.

Offer Apprentice Salary During Training. Apprentice salaries might be well below market rate but rapidly increase above market average as the officer gains experience, training, and credentials. This approach is effective as a retention tool and helps to attract trained officers from other departments (Orrick, 2008a). In light of developments in such cities as Portland, Oregon, where new hires are placed into a "preacademy," and apprenticeship and mentorship roles are developed even prior to enrollment, apprenticeship positions with pay are beginning to emerge as innovative strategies (Glanville, 2009).

Offer Educational Incentives. Educational incentives might be tied to mandatory service commitments as a posthire payback mechanism (Jackson et al., 2003). Carter and Sapp (1992) found that offering educational incentives might have been a pivotal moment in the professionalization of modern law enforcement by linking police practitioners to higher educational goals and expectations. Roberg and Bonn (2004) claim that tying educational incentives to recruitment efforts has multiple benefits beyond retention. Outside of policing, Moyle et al. (2003) found that educational incentives offered to enhance job satisfaction among nurses would also establish long-term relationships between nurses and hospitals. Strategies that embed tuition and educational incentives in apprenticeship contexts can help not only retain workers but also create solid linkages between school-based learning and career pathways (Cantor, 1997). The benefits of such outreach accrue by establishing linkages between personal educational fulfillment and mandated post-training service (Plecki et al., 2003; Jackson et al., 2003).

Create an Incentive Portfolio. Creating a portfolio of incentives, including compensation, bonuses, and loan and tuition reimbursement, can help improve retention (Kowal, Hassel, and Hassel, 2008). It can also benefit initial recruitment by targeting specific candidate populations, such as, for example, college-educated applicants through loan repayment programs. What separates these strategies from simply offering perks or buffet-style enticements is that the portfolio is generally tied to long-term candidate recruitment for specific groups (Kowal, Hassel, and Hassel, 2008).

Use Career Ladders. A career ladder can provide for vertical promotional advancement in an organization. It might take many forms. Career ladders can consist of establishing regular and open advancement and promotional opportunities, testing for open positions, and still other substantive steps allowing employee career advancement. Career laddering can also constitute internal structural changes to organizations, allowing employees freer access to upper rungs of a ladder of achievement (Prince, 2003; Sochalski, 2002). These opportunities can also have symbolic meaning, fostering professionalism by allowing for promotional advancement and responsiveness to employee needs and career ambition and reinforcing feelings that employees are engaged in a bona fide career (Bacharach, Conley, and Shedd, 1986; Staiger, Auerbach, and Buerhaus, 2000). Visible career ladders show employees multiple pathways to organizational success.

Both the formal and abstract characteristics of career ladders can positively affect employee perceptions of organizational commitment, professional orientation, and tangible opportunity for personal and professional improvement. Sochalski (2002) found that career ladders helped attract certified nurses not currently working in the profession back to the field. Fitzgerald (2006) found similar advancement opportunities to have benefits in retail and industrial work. Next-generation salary steps in many career ladders are integral in attracting 21st-century employees (Risher, 2002). Within policing, Orrick (2008a) suggests a dual-career track based on operational abilities (e.g., officer I, II, III) rather than supervision. This would supplement laddering with salary advancement based on nontraditional abilities. The Pasadena (California) Police Department's civilian career ladder provides employees mobility within the organization ("Q & A Chief Bernard Melekian," 2009). Career laddering disrupts the inertia inherent in many social-service organizations that can limit impressions of personal and career advancement (Rosenholtz, 1986; Spuck, 1974).

Agencies that adopt career ladders as a recruitment technique might strengthen the links between entry-level positions and future advancement opportunities. Some organizations have experimented with job zones based on education, experience, and projected growth metrics derived from needs assessments of targeted organizational growth (Prince, 2003). Supplemental management training for ladder climbers has been used to strengthen preparation of entry-level employees (Prince, 2003; Robinson, Murrells, and Clinton, 2006).

Consider Offering Perks—But Wisely. For the private sector, perks might be seen as a key retention (and recruitment) tool. Perks might be categorized as soft (e.g., ease of commute, challenge of work) or hard (e.g., flexible scheduling and promotional opportunities) (Shilling, 2004). For example, some of Google's benefits include on-site physician and dental care, free massage and yoga, free meals, a three-week vacation in the first year of employment, free recreation, an on-site car wash and dry cleaner, an on-site fitness facility, flexible work hours, and casual dress for nearly every employee (Switzer, 2006). Just as educational incentives can increase job satisfaction and human and social capital, so too can perks (Holtom, Mitchell, and Lee, 2006; Mitchell, Holtom, Lee, Sablynski, and Erez, 2001). Employee perceptions of these perks might be more directly related to positive organizational culture than to the actual benefits received. Perks should be integrated into a larger employee-retention plan to be most effective (Mitchell, Holtom, Lee, Sablynski, and Erez, 2001). Perks distributed to the entire organization with little discussion of their intent can be detrimental to an organization (Sigler, 1999).

Some research disputes the increase in productivity attributed to perks. Hausknecht, Rodda, and Howard (2008) call perks "investments" and relate them to longevity but found that they affected long-term employment for less than 10 percent of respondents in their survey. Some perks, such as profit-sharing in the private sector, can be altered to focus on group performance or adapted to other settings. Police departments, for example, can give a unit a day off for a job well done or increase its budget to reward exceptional performance. While not all private-sector benefits might be transferable to the public sector, the public sector can still offer unique perks (e.g., low-interest mortgage loans for officers).

Investigate Job Flexibility as a Plan with Multiple Personnel Benefits. Job flexibility—including such strategies as working from home, telecommuting, alternative scheduling, job-sharing, and staggered work hours—is gaining popularity in multiple work environments (Hill et al., 2001). The perception that such strategies allow for a better work and family balance is an attractive concept to workers and is supported by a host of empirical research on work-life balance and its influence on public health and individual happiness (Aronsson, 1999; Hill et al., 2001; Levin-Epstein, 2006; Sparks et al., 1997; Swanberg, 2005). As such, the impact of flexibility on job and overall company performance has been positive (Kogi, 1997; Perrons, 2000; Sánchez et al., 2007). M. Anderson and Gobeil (2003) found that, in 67 percent of cases, job flexibility strategies were "very effective" in improving employee retention in child-welfare service positions. Richman et al. (2008) note that both formal and informal flexibility boost retention times, particularly when seen as a product of organizational commitment to employee work-life balance. Eaton (2003) found that job-flexibility policies not only had a positive impact on overall retention but also helped attract young, family-oriented job prospects. A consistent theme in research on job flexibility concerns the obstacles to implementation that, if overcome, can offer a wide variety of benefits, including greater employee retention.

Increasing the availability of flexible work options, such as flexible hours, alternative work schedules, job-sharing, and part-time employment, allowing for employee choice in work structure is strongly related to reducing turnover (Lynch and Tuckey, 2004). Alternative work schedules also reduce sick time, absences, and overtime. Job-sharing, in which two employees hold a position together, require more employees and equipment, as well as organizational commitment to innovative job scheduling, and might not be desirable to all (Hill et al., 2001; Richman et al., 2008). Nevertheless, job-sharing and part-time scheduling have boosted retention of highly qualified nurses (O'Brien-Pallas, Duffield, and Alksnis, 2004) and information-technology and library-science professionals (Stanley, 2008).

For police, Pierce and Dunham (1992) found significant improvements in scheduling of personal activities after a departmental change from a forward-rotating eight-hour-shift schedule to a 12-hour compressed shift schedule. Agencies should identify what flexible scheduling and sharing options are already in place, identify employees' general and individual needs, examine what comparable agencies are providing, and then try to meet employees' group and individual needs and improve worker access to flexible work practices (Switzer, 2006; Lynch and Tuckey, 2004). Departments implementing flexible work practices will need to promote them among staff and train management to implement flexible solutions in each work area.

The organizational commitment to this strategy must be high in order to regulate the myriad administrative, payroll, benefit, and compensation issues that arise with job flexibility (Best, 1981). The organization might wish to conduct a preliminary feasibility study to determine costs and benefits of such a program (Meier, 1979).

Employee Engagement

Employee engagement refers to a number of strategies organizations might pursue to help employees balance work and career—what literature terms *life-task relationships* (Cartwright and Holmes, 2006; Jamrog, 2004). All strategies employed by organizations to address worker needs can be engaging. Employee-engagement strategies often emphasize affective outcomes, such as resolving employees' emotional needs, restoring trust, and increasing confidence that organizations care about their workers (Towers Perrin, 2003). *Engagement* in this sense means embracing an overall idea that companies have a responsibility to regulate employee self-efficacy, trust, and well-being.

Understand What "Engagement" Means and How to Create It. Employee engagement includes enhancing the diversity of work, allowing officers to have a voice in decisions, providing feedback, recognizing their achievement, creating opportunities to build cohesion, and instituting mentoring programs. The concept has shown success when applied to policing: The Santa Cruz Consolidated Emergency Communication Center experiences 1-percent turnover in an industry with an average attrition rate of 17 percent (Switzer, 2006). Its success is attributed to a willingness to try different approaches, listening to employees, engaging them in planning and decisionmaking, and recognizing good behavior.

Allow Employees to Experience Others' Duties Through Work Diversity. Assignment rotation can be a valuable way to provide opportunities for officers and deputies to experience special duties, thereby enhancing the diversity of their work (S. Lewis, Kagan, and Heaton, 2000; Palmer et al., 1998). Rotational assignments might be an employment incentive for younger employees entering law enforcement, but there are benefits for senior officers as well. Senior officers transferred for short periods might allow officers to break out of professional ruts while promoting cross-functional knowledge and experience. Similarly, cross-training might also increase job satisfaction and commitment to the organization (Davenport, Thomas, and Cantrell, 2002; Kirpal, 2004; Palmer et al., 1998).

Provide for Job Shadowing with New Hires and Beyond. Job shadowing can expose officers to other units, build their future aspirations, and create camaraderie among officers across shifts and duties. It might also enhance a deeper understanding for the integrated duties all have in the department, as when an inexperienced patrol officer shadows court security, narcotics enforcement, and investigating officers. Pairing new hires with mentors in shadowing and supervised contexts can strengthen skill development, coaching, organizational bonds, and occupational socialization (COPS, 2009b). It also inculcates a broader organizational mission with associated strategies for enhancing commitment and work progress (Luthans and Jensen, 2005). Shadowing and mentoring opportunities expand the organizational role in employee engagement by providing a supportive peer for new hires who might be simultaneously a leader and partner (Gunnels-Perry, 2007). Morgan and Kritsonis (2008) suggest that these relationships are crucial and essential and should be established immediately after hire.

Give Employees a Voice in Decisionmaking. When employees believe that they have a voice that can influence organizational decisions, it deepens their commitment to the organization and encourages ongoing feedback, creating a continuous, positive dialogue. Supervisors should listen to their officers and have personal one-on-one contact whenever possible. Police departments can increase officer input and feedback through carefully crafted surveys about organizational effectiveness (Cartwright and Holmes, 2006; Towers Perrin, 2003). This type of input can be effective so long as the department is willing to act on the results. The chief of the Washington, D.C., Metropolitan Police Department, for example, claims that allowing officers to be more engaged with their work helped halve attrition rates (see box, next page).

Allow for Employee Feedback, and Make it Meaningful. Providing feedback is critical, especially for younger-generation workers. A 360-degree evaluation, in which workers are evaluated by managers, colleagues, subordinates, and clients, has shown promise in integrating employee feedback in meaningful ways. Several studies (Hazucha, Hezlett, and Schneider, 1993; London and Wohlers, 1991; A. Walker and Smither, 1999) indicate that the use of 360-degree evaluation helps improve performance by maximizing the utility of feedback for promotions, advancement, and compensation. Orrick (2008a) states that feedback should be timely, specific, and job related. Supervisors should be as specific as possible about strategies officers can use to improve performance.

Improving Recruitment and Retention Through Employee Engagement

The Washington Metropolitan Police Department, with approximately 3,800 officers, is among the largest in the nation. In addition to facing many of the same challenges that other large urban agencies do, the department, given its jurisdiction in the nation's capital, has several unique responsibilities requiring personnel with a wide variety of skills and interests. Maintaining this staff, according to Cathy Lanier (2008), chief of the department, requires a focus on both recruitment and retention.

To make itself more appealing to new recruits, the department seeks to instill a sense of pride in its history, portraying itself as providing an environment in which recruits will want to work. The department benefits, Lanier claims, both from the opportunities it can offer as a large department and from its unique location.

Lanier claims that, when she became chief, the department had a monthly attrition rate of about 20 officers but that allowing officers to be more engaged with their work cut that rate nearly in half (J. Wilson and Grammich, 2009a). One example of employee engagement Lanier cites is a website on "chief concerns," permitting officers to anonymously suggest ways to make their job easier and improve the department. The chief publicly recognizes suggestions that the organization has implemented, encouraging officers to make further suggestions. Lanier contends that officers who are more engaged are more likely to stay with the agency.

Positive behaviors can be modeled in training and demonstrations with other officers. Research consistently shows a strong relationship between feedback and organizational commitment (Cangelosi, Markham, and Bounds, 1998; Eskildsen and Nussler, 2000; Saari and Judge, 2004).

Discussing positive and negative performance with employees should not be postponed until a formally scheduled performance appraisal but should be reviewed immediately. Samuel Walker (2006) found that performance evaluation procedures in policing have been criticized and that there is insufficient research to support their utility and efficacy as a feedback mechanism. A 1977 Police Foundation study found that performance appraisals did not adequately reflect police work and generally provided inflated assessments of officer performance (Landy, 1977). A 1997 report found that little progress had been made in improving on these failures in the 20 years since the Landy report (Oettmeier and Wycoff, 1997). Providing feedback is essential, but confining it to procedural evaluations might prove to have little effect on officer self-efficacy and turnover.

Recognize Employees' Successes. Behavior that is recognized is more likely to be repeated. Orrick (2008a) contends that employee recognition is a process, not a singular event, and can occur at many levels: direct supervisors, upper-level management, and the community or other authorities can all participate in recognizing officer success. Letters of commendation, achievement, and recognition, as well as simple thank-you notes, can help show that good work has been recognized. Other more-elaborate approaches include conducting morale or pride meetings, which allow for social interaction and improving communication, trust, and identification with fellow employees (Orrick, 2008a). Budgeting for small tokens can reinforce good behavior, creating additional rewards for the agency while supporting positive morale within the department. Posting compliments of the department and officers can provide encouragement for the whole department. Having high-performing officers meet with and be recognized by external city officials can promote the department as a whole while recognizing individuals and units and publicize the good work of the department to others in the community (Orrick, 2008a). Even gathering informally to celebrate birthdays or anniversaries, host team-building activities (such as sports contests), or watch sporting events can offer opportunities to recognize success (Stairs et al., 2006).

The keys to effective recognition are timeliness (Kim, 2005), sincerity (Luthans, 2000), selectivity (Del Bueno, 1993; Luthans, 2000), and substance (Enz and Siguaw, 2000). These are crucial, as improper implementation can backfire by creating or contributing to a culture of phony praise, indiscriminate recognition, and meaningless ceremony. Effective recognition, by contrast, can build a more-meaningful connection between employee and management that is rooted in organizational culture (Lloyd Morgan, undated; Rust et al., 1996). Orrick (2008a) also suggests that these strategies can positively influence employees from different generations, all of whom desire individual recognition and engagement.

Mentor Officers Beyond the Field Training Experience. Private-sector companies have long mentored new employees, with such practices regarded as the cornerstone of any organizational commitment to employee retention in multiple fields (Butler and Felts, 2006; Hegstad and Wentling, 2004; Ingersoll and Smith, 2003; Musser, 2001; Smith and Ingersoll, 2004). Peer mentorship can promote a wide variety of long-term goals, including collegial relationships among employees (Smith and Ingersoll, 2004), professional development and on-the-job skill retention (Greene and Puetzer, 2002), employee engagement (Kickul, 2002), occupational socialization (Hurst and Koplin-Baucum, 2003), and positive morale, loyalty, and job satisfaction (Ingersoll and Smith, 2003). These strategies are particularly helpful in establishing strong relationships between beginning employees and experienced mentors for minority workers (Friedman and Holtom, 2002; Musser, 2001; COPS, 2009b) and in difficult-to-fill positions in rural areas. While mentoring programs can be relatively inexpensive tools to retain employees, their success depends on the professionalism and confidentiality practiced by those involved, as well as the department's commitment to training mentors (L. Lee, 2001; Switzer, 2006).

There is little empirical research on the effectiveness of mentoring programs in police organizations. Orrick (2008a) identifies some intervening and confounding variables that complicate the assessment of mentoring programs. These include the subjective nature of mentoring (making it hard to quantify), the specificity of individual goals, and varied levels of mentor and mentee experience, commitment, and ability. Agencies can track participants, surveying their satisfaction and monitoring them over time. Field training evaluation structures can be extended to mentoring.

Research in other fields shows that mentoring can succeed. A one-year longitudinal quasi-experiment on the effectiveness of a formal mentoring program at a Fortune 100 corporation found that employees who participated in the program reported significantly higher levels of job satisfaction than did a control group without a mentor (Seibert, 1999). Similarly, a study of mentoring programs for new teachers found that those with mentors from the same subject field, who participated in such activities as planning and collaboration with other teachers, were less likely to move to other schools or to leave the teaching occupation after their first year (Smith and Ingersoll, 2004). Other research finds like of ,and satisfaction and contact with, mentors were higher when protégés perceived themselves to be more similar to their mentors. Actual race pairing was related to protégé perceptions of the amount of career support and to how well mentors liked protégés (Ensher and Murphy, 1997).

Improving Organizational Effectiveness

Communicate Departmental Goals Routinely and Effectively. Be Fair and Transparent in All Aspects of Departmental Policy. Reduce Unnecessary Bureaucracy. Select and Maintain an Effective Management and Supervisory Staff. A major reason for turnover is the perceived quality of supervision. The relationship that immediate and midlevel supervisors have with their officers has the most influence on an officer's decision to stay or leave the department (Orrick, 2008a, 2008b). The way police departments select supervisors and leaders, often by longevity or superior performance in operational positions (as opposed to management potential), results in poor supervisory training and mentorship for police supervisors, as well as disconnection from line-level officers. Given this, police departments must hire well, promote well, provide comprehensive training, and hold leaders accountable (Orrick, 2008a).

A study of resignations and transfers in ten United Kingdom police forces found that, when asked about ways to improve the service, respondents emphasized the need to increase support from all levels of management, as well as reduce paperwork and bureaucracy (Christine Cooper and Ingram, 2004). Officers' perceptions that management was unfair and ineffective at all levels led to increased resignations and transfers. A study of police in Australia concluded that departments should focus on improving management style and communication, as well as provide training for supervisors and managers on key management topics (Lynch and Tuckey, 2004). Effective law-enforcement leadership development programs improve the leader's ability to achieve organizational goals that serve the public and enhance their ability to develop individuals, teams, and organization for the future (Moriarty 2009; Orrick, 2008a).

Conclusion

Improving retention can not only boost department morale but also save costs for replacing personnel. Among the costs associated with turnover are those for recruiting, selecting, and training new employees, and those associated with loss of productivity and knowledge. These costs, especially those for recruiting and training, can be higher for police agencies than for other employers.

To improve retention, departments should understand who is likely to leave, when they are likely to leave, and their reasons for doing so. Younger officers, other new officers, and women and minority officers leave policing in disproportionate numbers. Officers might leave for many reasons, including the following:

- other opportunities elsewhere
- better compensation, including salary, benefits, viable career ladders, and adequate training and equipment
- personality traits and characteristics, with those having high levels of anxiety being more likely to leave
- organizational issues, such as supervisory practices
- employee needs for feedback and recognition, a stimulating work environment, and job satisfaction.

Agencies can undertake a wide variety of initiatives to improve retention or to minimize the detrimental effects of attrition. These include planning and analysis of employee needs, reducing the financial impact of attrition, enhancing compensation and perks, engaging employees to improve the agency, and improving organizational effectiveness through open communication and fair and transparent practices.

Few of these strategies have been empirically tested. Little but anecdotes is known about many of them. The application of these strategies must be evaluated empirically to determine whether they actually improve officer retention. Surveying officers pre- and posthire, conducting analyses of departmental attrition data, collecting data about supervisor and management impressions of these programs, or evaluating the workplace environment in a qualitative manner might indicate success or room for improvement. There is also little discussion across agencies regarding the different strategies each has employed and the prospects for success they see in their own organizations. To date, the literature is rich with ideas, many of which have showed promise in other fields. Police departments can begin to experiment with these and other strategies but should incorporate mechanisms to assess their effectiveness.

CHAPTER FOUR

Recruitment: Filling the Bucket

Throughout the 2000s, police-officer recruitment has concerned police executives and administrators from agencies of varying size and locale. Early in the decade, the nation's largest agencies, including those in Chicago, New York, and Los Angeles, reported problems recruiting qualified applicants (Butterfield, 2001). Half of all agencies and two-thirds of those serving at least 50,000 residents also reported staffing problems stemming from a lack of qualified applicants (Koper, Maguire, and Moore, 2001). In 2004, California police chiefs identified recruitment and retention as their second-most pressing issue, trailing only funding (California Police Chiefs Association, 2004) and reflecting concerns of earlier years (California Police Chiefs Association 1994, 2001). Even as recent economic conditions have led to an increased number of applications, police departments might still find a shortage of applicants qualified for their work (Castro, 2009; Chambers, 2009).

Identifying sources of the recruiting challenge remains problematic because symptoms might vary by jurisdiction. Nevertheless, departments can identify dimensions and categorize them as external to policing, such as economic and social conditions and work-life changes, or specific to the profession or specific departments, such as low pay or benefits. Many of these issues are evident in our bucket metaphor. In this chapter, we focus on the recruitment challenge in policing and on detailing specific strategies evident in the literature from several disciplines for recruiting the best available candidates.

The recruitment challenge appears to be deepening over time, as generational preferences and conceptions of work, and career change and as other trends, work to reduce the pool of qualified applicants. Whereas agencies have had historical difficulties recruiting women and minority applicants, their inability to grapple with generational differences has shown the profession to be underprepared for the rapidly changing and uncertain economic and social landscape (Jordan et al., 2009; Orrick, 2008a; J. Wilson and Grammich, 2009a). Previously unconsidered issues, such as the pull of more-lucrative careers and negative images of policing, might further deplete the applicant pool, particularly as the economy improves over time (Cavanagh, 2003; Koper, Maguire, and Moore, 2001; Flynn, 2000).

The recruitment challenge is a product of several rapidly changing trends, which departments appear ill-prepared to address, in the way police recruiters and potential applicants view each other. Absent organized recruitment programs, objectives, or strategies, police departments have placed themselves at a growing disadvantage in recruiting qualified officers, losing them to other industries and fields at a quickening rate (Scrivner, 2006; Taylor et al., 2006).

Concerns about recruiting minorities and women that dominated police recruitment discussions decades ago have now expanded to concerns that the profession is failing to market itself to a new generation of workers (COPS, 2009b). Personnel costs comprise 75 to 85 percent of police department budgets, underscoring the importance of hiring, recruiting, and selecting the best candidates, even in uncertain times (Orrick, 2008a; White and Escobar, 2008). Agencies have little guidance for recruitment strategies, so difficulties persist. Jordan et al. (2009) found that only one in five agencies had targeted recruitment strategies for women and minorities. White and Escobar (2008, p. 120) lament police agencies' unwillingness to "sell themselves" when recruiting for diversity. As the diversity and breadth of the communities that agencies serve expands, agencies might face difficulties in recruiting officers for positions that are increasingly complex, require new competencies, or require interaction with communities whose needs they do not always know or understand.

Many departments have answered the recruiting challenge by expanding their recruitment efforts. Orrick (2008a) illustrates why recruitment programs, selection processes, and screening techniques are essential in a broader, proactive plan. Facing mounting uncertainty about staffing deficiencies, organizations should first assess their needs. In this chapter, we describe how to create and use such an assessment to construct a recruitment strategy that meets individual agency needs, how to improve selection and recruiting processes, and how these strategies might help departments navigate the recruitment challenge. We begin by briefly reviewing the history of police recruitment.

Police Recruitment Practices: Past and Present

In 1931, the National Committee on Law Observation and Enforcement (commonly known as the Wickersham Commission), appointed by President Herbert Hoover to study enforcement of Prohibition, detailed advances needed in the professionalization of policing, including the elimination of the spoils system for recruitment and hiring (Alpert, 1991; S. Walker, 1997). As police agencies moved toward merit-based hiring in the 1940s and 1950s, the dual problems of liability for law-enforcement behavior and increasing concerns over discrimination in police work fueled the use of more-scientific methods, such as psychometrics and standardized psychological testing in recruitment (Fyfe et al., 1997; Hogue, Black, and Sigler, 1994). These culminated in the formation of the Law Enforcement Assistance Administration (LEAA) in 1967, which sought to implement Equal Employment Opportunity Commission guidelines in the hiring of law-enforcement officers (Scrivner, 2006). The LEAA aligned selection methods with perceived job duties to create more-valid external analyses of demonstrated skills for police work. By the end of the 1960s, agencies nationwide used scientific and career-specific methods of testing, evaluating, and examining potential recruits on the basis of departmental perceptions of what one needed to know to be a good police officer.

This system was challenged in the mid-1970s, when Goldstein (1977) examined what police did on patrol. He found that most officer time in uniform was spent in human-service roles, such as helping citizens, negotiating disputes, or interacting with diverse community members in nonenforcement roles. The skills required for this work were incompatible with those for which recruits were screened, trained, and tested. This realization led to a reorientation of police work toward community policing. The Commission on Accreditation for Law Enforcement Agencies put forth recommendations for diversifying personnel to reflect the community (White and Escobar, 2008), although selection practices remained inconsistent with the new police role into the 1980s.

Evaluation processes might either "select out" candidates (that is, discern flaws in a candidate disqualifying him or her from a position) or "select in" candidates (that is, identify positive qualities that make an applicant an attractive candidate). Controversies over the two approaches and their merit have persisted since the advent of the community-policing era (Scrivner, 2006). It is unclear what skills agencies should identify in "selecting in" candidates, given rapid changes in community needs and demographics (Canadian Association of Chiefs of Police et al., 2000; Woska, 2006). The "selecting out" or hurdle process of recruitment remains attractive because many agencies cling to an outdated perception of the police role (Scrivner, 2006).

Nevertheless, rigidity is giving way to some experimentation and innovation. The Community Policing Consortium, through its Hiring in the Spirit of Service program, has sought to align hiring practices with individual agency needs regarding officer duties and skills. The results might help agencies attract a wider range of officers for open positions (Scrivner, 2006). The use of assessment centers and hurdle approaches might be incompatible with career needs and goals of new generations of recruits (DeCicco, 2000; Orrick, 2008a; Taylor et al., 2006). At best, the current climate of police recruitment consists of a lack of uniformity, little widespread use of data or research to guide recruitment efforts, and a fragmented approach to understanding the crisis and planning a response to it (Orrick, 2008a; Scrivner, 2006; White and Escobar, 2008).

How these fractured approaches have affected recruiting in recent years is unclear. Strawbridge and Strawbridge (1990) provided one of the first systematic efforts to describe the recruitment environment across jurisdictions, surveying 72 local police departments with 500 or more sworn officers about their recruiting, screening, and training practices. Among their findings was the need for a computerized database to facilitate communication about best practices given societal changes and resource limitations.

Langworthy, Hughes, and Sanders (1995) conducted a second survey of 60 of these agencies in 1994. They found decreasing use of television for recruiting, of maximum age requirements, of preemployment standards, and of state subsidies for training. They also found increased use of intelligence tests, psychological reviews, and duration of academy training and little change in probationary periods.

Taylor et al. (2006) conducted a national survey of nearly 1,000 agencies in 2002, including 32 of those in the earlier survey by Strawbridge and Strawbridge. They found little evidence to accept or reject hypotheses of a growing "cop crunch" but did find that some of these agencies had developed a severe shortage of officers, with more than 10 percent of their allocated slots vacant. They also found that many agencies had developed targeted recruiting strategies for minority, female, veteran, college-grad, and experienced candidates, but that they had difficulties in hiring sufficient numbers of female and minority candidates.

Determining Staffing Needs

Agencies must prepare themselves for hiring by first assessing their staffing needs (Switzer, 2006). There has been little analysis on the determination of staffing needs, despite the belief that empirical analyses of organizational needs would have widespread benefit. Police needs assessments have their roots in patrol allocation formulas of the pre–community policing era, when patrol manpower and risk formulas relied heavily on crime activity and calls for service as standard measurements of patrol saturation (Larson, 1978; Metropolitan Atlanta Crime Commission, 1977). As policing has grown more complex, staffing analyses have evolved as well. The Delaware State Personnel Office (2002) recommended the use of internal assessments prior to hiring and training law-enforcement employees. The National Institute of Corrections (Liebert and Miller, 2001) published a guidebook for corrections facilities that assisted facilities in conducting staffing analyses. Orrick (2008a) has also supported the use of needs analysis in determining hiring levels. In an applied example, the Pinal County (Ariz.) Sheriff's Office (PCSO) conducted an internal staffing analysis that examined such topics as patrol deployment, attrition rates, and scheduling policy to determine future hiring needs (PCSO, 2008). These and other strategies form a broad organizational needs assessment that can help shape the hiring process. The steps we discuss in this section, derived from organizational-assessment literature on strategic planning, might help focus and set the parameters for a strategic hiring plan. Many of these strategies can be performed internally, without external assistance.

Develop an Assessment Team. Staffing decisions and processes involve the input of community, government, and department stakeholders. Involving them in an assessment team invigorates hiring with input from those affected by hiring decisions. Departments might also wish to consider using outside agencies or private companies to assist with the needs assessment, which will come at a cost but can add expertise, objectivity, and independence. Orrick (2008a) suggests that assembling the assessment team could be as crucial in the hiring process as enacting the hiring plan itself. By choosing a team that represents all stakeholders in the hiring process, the department can assess its true needs and make more-comprehensive decisions about staffing.

Identify Budget and Source of Revenue. Analyzing available revenue is seen as a final step in conducting a needs assessment of hiring in corrections (Clem, Krauth, and Wenger, 2000) but might be better used as an initial step in police staffing assessments. Evaluating resources can help departments realistically determine their true capacities for personnel expansion (Clem, Krauth, and Wenger, 2000).

Specify Organizational Goals and Values. Hiring criteria differ by region and organizational setting (Kahanov and Andrews, 2001). There might also be variation within a single department, with upper management, training staff, and line-level officers all having different ideas. Defining candidate characteristics should be a deliberative process. It might involve the creation or reiteration of a value or mission statement communicating a department's core beliefs (Switzer, 2006). Crafting the "ideal" candidate should be tied closely to organizational goals and mission and help establish criteria the department will use to hire (Orrick, 2008a).

Use Benchmarks to Determine True Staffing Need. Despite the use of data-driven peer comparisons to determine police behavior in such areas as police growth and personnel expenditures, benchmarks determining staffing needs have not improved on informal peer comparisons (Nalla, Lynch, and Leiber, 1997). A few analyses have used hard data: The PCSO analysis used five other agencies of comparable size, patrol strength, and demography for a staffing comparison (PCSO, 2008). Similarly, a Canadian policing human-resource study used computer models to project attrition rates and models to predict police staffing requirements (Canadian Association of Chiefs of Police et al., 2000). Using benchmarks for staffing needs requires data collection and analysis, but these could be data readily available to most departments, including those on demographics, budgetary outlays, political structure, crime trends, calls for service, and community needs (Koper, Maguire, and Moore, 2001; Orrick, 2008a). The benchmarks could then be adjusted for qualitative differences, such as by emphasis on discretionary time for community policing and problem-solving projects. Additionally, a performance- or workload-based assessment can be conducted for an individual agency to estimate the number of officers required to meet workload demands (Shane, 2007; Fritsch, Liederbach, and Taylor, 2009). Such models can empirically account for discretionary and relief (e.g., authorized leave) time, as well as work schedules and minimum staffing requirements. It is common for agencies to consult with staffing experts to conduct these analyses, although various staffing software programs are available to assist those that prefer to conduct such analyses internally.

Integrate the Community in the Hiring Process. In addition to department stakeholders, including community input can better inform decisions on external issues (Switzer, 2006). Community members can help ensure that hiring reflects not only community needs but also community characteristics. Orrick (2008a) sees community input as crucial to determining standards for hiring. Scrivner (2006) recognizes the essential input of minority community members for establishing ethnic diversity in a department. The city of St. Paul, Minnesota, as part of a program to reduce racially biased policing, worked with the community to determine a list of characteristics (e.g., enthusiastic, fair, possessed of good judgment, tenacious, respectful, compassionate, unafraid to engage the community) that ideal candidates should possess (McDevitt, Farrell, and Wolf, 2008). Without a clearer picture of community character and an assessment of the needs of special populations in a department's jurisdiction, benchmark comparisons might omit community viewpoints not reflected in raw data. Community leaders, seeing that the department is inclusive of community input and needs, might "recruit" for the department by speaking positively of careers with it (Haggerty, 2009; Whetstone, Reed, and Turner, 2006).

Attracting Candidates: Considerations

Organizations must consider several issues for attracting candidates. First, they should understand the function of research and data-gathering in the personnel selection process (Switzer, 2006; Canadian Association of Chiefs of Police et al., 2000; Chien and Chen, 2008). This can inform each aspect of the process by examining it as a larger endeavor of matching individual talents to departmental goals and objectives. Second, they should craft recruitment goals that reflect an ethic that is visible to applicants (McKay and Avery, 2005; Orrick, 2008a). Decision rules about qualities of good candidates should spring from the department's climate as revealed in the earliest stages of the needs assessment and be linked to the attraction strategy. Third, when examining strategies for attracting candidates, departments should remember that the relative success of strategies might depend on budget, departmental commitment, personnel resources for recruitment, and departmental effectiveness in targeting specific subgroups that the agency seeks to recruit.

There might be synergies among these strategies (Switzer, 2006). When the community and department stakeholders have formed a partnership, identified hiring resources and needs, and used research to inform their work, the hiring process might flow more smoothly, with specific strategies that "work" for the department arising from the outflow of ideas, philosophy, and planning.

Attracting Candidates: Internal Strategies

The best recruiters for a department are often its own personnel (Baker and Carrera, 2007; Haggerty, 2009). Building professional networks within the department to support recruitment can enhance community outreach efforts by making recruitment an overall philosophy rather than a task to be performed. Internal strategies that emphasize interaction, relationship-building, and partnerships with the public can enhance perceptions of diversity and boost hiring of women and minorities (Taylor et al., 2006; COPS, 2009b). Without a climate that reflects legitimate and credible organizational beliefs, recruitment for diversity can be seen as false and might even increase turnover (McKay and Avery, 2005). Having a department-wide outlook that emphasizes recruitment potential in public interactions can help overcome negative or unrealistic impressions of what police work entails and contribute to a larger strategic recruitment plan. Recruiting can become a part of the department's everyday interactions with the public (Baker and Carrera, 2007; Canadian Association of Chiefs of Police et al., 2000).

Build Employee Referral Networks. Referrals by family, friends, and employees strongly influence individual decisions to apply for careers in public service (Baker and Carrera, 2007; Switzer, 2006; Slater and Reiser, 1988; Yearwood, 2003). Relationship-based recruiting can also dispel myths about police work and build associations across different groups (Baker and Carrera, 2007). Applicants who are referred and sponsored by an existing employee are more likely to complete the hiring process (Barber, 1998).

Two important influences on the decision to apply for police positions are department reputation and exposure to the variety of tasks that police perform; these can be solidified with employee referrals and community activism (Baker and Carrera, 2007; Slater and Reiser, 1988). Personal referrals can also provide a realistic portrayal of how a law-enforcement career affects family life (Ryan et al., 2001). To boost referrals, departments should consider compensation and other incentives for them (Switzer, 2006; Haggerty, 2009; Lachnit, 2001). Relationship-based and employee referral strategies help increase applicant pools and provide balance to other recruitment strategies, such as online processes, that lack human interaction.

Create a Department Recruitment Unit. A recruitment unit can be separate from recruitment teams that perform hiring needs assessments or linked interdepartmentally (Geis and Cavanagh, 1966; Orrick, 2008a; Whetstone, Reed, and Turner, 2006). Recruitment units oversee internal and external strategies devoted to recruitment, such as testing, advertising, coordinating outreach programs, media relations, and recruiting events (New York City Commission to Combat Police Corruption, 2008). By establishing such a unit, departments can better ensure that recruitment efforts reflect the department's needs, goals, and philosophies and enhance the credibility and openness of recruitment efforts (Breaugh and Starke, 2000). Departments should consider structuring the team and mentoring team members so as to best improve quality and efficacy; this can include integrating background investigative and personnel staff into the recruitment team (Switzer, 2006; Lim et al., 2009). Departments should also consider using incentives for recruiting-team participation and success (Switzer, 2006; Whetstone, Reed, and Turner, 2006).

Look Within the Department for Potential Recruits. Referral networks might consider a department's civilian staff for sworn positions, a strategy that would create "feeder" networks of existing employees (Ridgeway et al., 2008). Auxiliary and reserve ranks have frequently been used as an internal personnel resource (Yearwood, 2003). Because such employees are already part of the organization, this process reduces hiring costs, time, and procedures (Jordan et al., 2009).

Conduct an Internal Assessment of Employee-Engagement Strategies. Google, the Internet search-engine company, publishes a list of benefits called the "I bet you don't have that where you work" list (Sullivan, 2005). The list details Google's employee-engagement strategies, which range from perks (on-site dry cleaning, a wine club, and yoga classes) to more-traditional benefits (flexible hours, vacation benefits, and health counseling). Police agencies should ask themselves what they present that will attract the best possible officers. Police chiefs should ask themselves, "Why would I want to work for this department?" (McKeever and Kranda, 2000). Conducting an inventory of benefits can be the first step in assessing those that work best in attracting candidates, those that are weak, and how they appear from the applicant's perspective. This is a crucial step in department marketing and outreach efforts (Orrick, 2008a). An inventory of benefits can also bolster department pride in recruiters who speak to candidates. The inventory could be conducted both to attract candidates and to prevent turnover (Switzer, 2006; Jordan et al., 2009; Sullivan, 2005).

Attracting Candidates: Outreach Strategies

Departments have used myriad outreach strategies over time to attract candidates. Though there is minimal research on their effectiveness, to attract candidates, departments have used such tools as advertise-and-wait, "word of mouse" social networking, traditional job fairs, and proactive community partnerships.

Use Internet Media in a Variety of Forms. Increasing use of the Internet has lured agencies seeking to attract officers. The interactive potential of Internet media has increased beyond simple advertising, and it continues to do so in ways that outpace empirical study (Russell, 2007). Websites have been seen as the top tool in attracting qualified applicants (Switzer, 2006). Internet presence should maximize department resources. The Los Angeles Police Department (LAPD) recruitment website contributed to an increase in recruitment during a fiscal year in which advertising budgets were cut (Lim et al., 2009). The democratic properties of the Internet have helped smaller agencies compete with larger ones for candidates (McKeever and Kranda, 2000). Nevertheless, use of the Internet only to place advertisements online and without any overall marketing strategy can be ineffective (Yearwood, 2003).

Many organizations have failed to jump the digital divide to best reach new generations of technologically savvy applicants. More than two-thirds of companies responding in one survey had never used social-networking sites in recruitment efforts, although nearly half said they searched such sites for information on applicants ("MySpace," 2006).

Contemporary Internet tools (referred to as *Web 2.0*) have magnified the importance of "word-of-mouse" tactics that new generations expect in their job search (Van Hoye and Lievens, 2007; Verhoeven,

Mashood, and Chansarkar, 2009). Social-networking sites, such as Facebook, MySpace, and Twitter (along with law-enforcement networking sites, such as Officer.com and Police Link), have increased in use but represent the social cornerstone of many young persons' lives (Russell, 2007). These websites enable connections across audiences, including high-school and college students and graduates, military personnel, professionals, former and current law enforcement, police supervisors, and job searchers from other fields ("MySpace," 2006; Van Hoye and Lievens, 2007; Verhoeven, Mashood, and Chansarkar, 2009). Podcasts, blogs, and "really simple syndication" (RSS) feeds have increased job-seekers' sophistication, allowing them to process growing amounts of information and network more efficiently (Kolbitsch and Maurer, 2006; Martin, Reddington, and Kneafsey, 2009; Orrick, 2008a).

The Internet's overall effect on police recruiting varies, but agencies using it have been able to present their organizations in ways that influence applicants (Cable and Yu, 2006), dispel negative images (Ellis et al., 2005; Orrick, 2008a; Syrett and Lammiman, 2004) and transmit positive ones (Ellis et al., 2005; Verhoeven, Mashood, and Chansarkar, 2009), showcase their technological abilities (Charrier, 2000), and place recruiting efforts in contexts that resonate with new generations of applicants (Gubbins and Garavan, 2008). Despite the generational differences that might separate police command staff from young recruits, using Internet media could sell policing in messages that are heard very personally in a medium that previous generations might find impersonal (COPS, 2009b).

Use Electronic Media Other Than the Internet. Electronic recruitment techniques are not confined to blogs and websites. Gaming and other visual technology can also help attract new generations of recruits. Many simulation-based video games mimic interactive problem-solving activities, such as probing and telescoping, exploratory analysis, and critical thinking (Harrison, 2007). Beyond games, the use of emotional video clips in a structured, reality-show format can also help attract candidates (Lim et al., 2009). Interactive electronic media restructure traditional communications with workers, which could be a boon to departments with advanced technological capabilities (Ellis et al., 2005; Harrison, 2007). Yet, use of electronic media can present a paradox: If emotional vignettes of police life are used to attract candidates, specifically where department diversity and work life are represented, the department must ensure that such representations and "simulations" are consistent with the realities of police work in their department.

Brand Your Department and Your Profession. The message transmitted through advertising media constitutes the "brand" that applicants see and the identity that agencies give themselves. In the first episode of the LAPD's Internet-based recruitment video series, a variety of images designed to present information to recruits include a black female police sergeant, a diverse workforce of Hispanic and Asian officers, and fast-paced and adventurous police work (LAPD, undated). These and other branding images attempt to foster a deep, emotional attachment to the department and its supposed values (in this case, opportunities for advancement and diversity for minority populations) through the use of a reality-based film clip directed to a younger audience (Orrick, 2008a; Sartain and Schumann, 2006). Aside from marketing a department image or philosophy, branding also sells the profession of policing by aligning positive impressions of police work with applicants who might feel a "calling" to human-service careers (Ellis et al., 2005; Scrivner, 2006; Slater and Reiser, 1988; COPS, 2009b). In the LAPD video, segments display officers attempting to calm disputes, dealing with family problems, and working closely with community members in emotionally charged situations as much as they display traditional "crime-fighter" images (LAPD, undated). These reality-based images are expected to resonate with Internet-savvy and video-oriented applicants who are seen as socially aware, brand-loyal, and susceptible to cause branding (Syrett and Lammiman, 2004). Branding in this way must be sincere and emotionally consistent with police work, or the department runs the risk of appearing out of touch with its intended audience (McKay and Avery, 2005; J. Wilson and Grammich, 2009a).

Use Community Liaisons to Reach Potential Recruits. Community liaison efforts have been a cornerstone of many community-policing strategies for decades, with notable impact on recruitment of diverse populations (Skolnick and Bayley, 1988). These liaisons need not be involved in direct recruitment efforts. Liaisons could be any employees conducting community outreach, especially with targeted populations.

Liaisons can be embedded in many ways. The Detroit Police Department's Recruiting Ambassadors program uses not only departmental employees but also community representatives for its recruitment effort, with incentives for community "ambassadors" to help recruit (Scrivner, 2006; Haggerty, 2009). Liaisons are often a critical part of outreach efforts to reach diverse populations but can also reflect diversity within the department in the eyes of potential candidates (Switzer, 2006). Liaison visibility and subsequent community relationships can enhance recruitment efforts with female candidates (Donnelly, 2005; Harrington, 2000) and in traditionally hard-to-reach ethnic and religious communities, such as Arab Americans (OJP, 2008), and other isolated urban populations (Cunningham and Wagstaff, 2006).

Open Department Doors and Allow On-Site Visits. Community policing can improve community visibility and, in turn, bolster recruitment efforts (Haggerty, 2009). When community partnerships are merely superficial, they risk alienating applicants who might be aware of hypocrisy in branding and advertising when such activities are inconsistent with realities of the job (Syrett and Lammiman, 2004). Outreach must be meaningful, genuine, and reflect a departmental desire to build true relationships with future employees (Baker and Carrera, 2007; Switzer, 2006; McKeever and Kranda, 2000). Realistic job-preview strategies, by providing accurate representations of the department, can influence a candidate's interest in an organization (McKay and Avery, 2005). Making outreach partnerships sincere requires going beyond traditional public appearances and might require imaginative techniques, such as site visits, to enhance connections with targeted populations (McKay and Avery, 2006). Such tactics can enhance applicant interest beyond initial attraction stages (Breaugh, 2008; Rynes, Bretz, and Gerhart, 1991) and might be particularly important for recruiting female and minority candidates when such persons occupy important positions within the agency (Avery and McKay, 2006; COPS, 2009b). Nevertheless, site visits that expose work climate, employee demographics, and physical environments that differ from department recruitment media can reduce interest (Breaugh, 2008). Agencies should make the interactions between candidates and staff meaningful and take the time to introduce important individuals within the department to the applicants.

Attend Career and Job Fairs. Face-to-face interaction and fostering human connections can make recruitment more meaningful and personal for both the department and applicants (Whetstone, Reed, and Turner, 2006). Many of these opportunities are available through local college and university placement offices and in military and civilian settings (Orrick, 2008a). Attending job and career fairs is often an expense for the department involving travel and creative marketing techniques for mixed results, although maximizing these opportunities can pay off in departmental visibility and recruit targeting (Switzer, 2006; Whetstone, Reed, and Turner, 2006; Yearwood, 2003). One potential benefit for departments attending such events is gaining firsthand insight on employment trends and overall staffing outlook in peer agencies; one drawback is that job fairs are largely limited to applicants currently looking for work (Breaugh, 2008).

Consider the Greater Value of Youth Programs in Recruiting. Explorer programs, internships through local schools, cadet academies, and mentorships with youth foster special relationships between young adults and departments (Whetstone, Reed, and Turner, 2006; Yearwood, 2003). From the development of the Department of Justice's Police Corps in the mid-1990s through the diffusion of similar scholarship, education, and training programs nationwide, youth outreach efforts have been a tradition of law-enforcement organizations.

Nevertheless, for many reasons, these efforts often produce few results for recruiting. Most youths entering policing decide prior to their high-school graduation to do so (Switzer, 2006; Slater and Reiser, 1988). Consequently, results for recruitment efforts vary widely (Whetstone, Reed, and Turner, 2006; Yearwood, 2003). Costly and time-intensive efforts, such as Explorer programs, might misdirect resources that could be used to entice undecided youths.

Beyond identifying specific candidates, such programs brand the profession for young persons in the community (Presman, Chapman, and Rosen, 2002; Ridgeway et al., 2008). They might also acquaint the department with newer generations of applicants, including their work-life preferences, expectations, and career visions. By forging partnerships with a wide variety of youth, the value of such programs might extend beyond recruiting. At the same time, such programs help those already contemplating a police career develop qualifications within a police organization (COPS, 2009b).

Target Second-Career Applicants, but Assess and Train Them Appropriately. With the economic downturn of the late 2000s, some police departments noted an increase in applicants seeking a second career in policing, emerging from fields as diverse as automobile manufacturing, steel fabrication, marketing, and business administration (Crowe, 2009; Currier, 2009). The Virginia State Police noted a surge in applications of individuals laid off from private-sector jobs in 2009, a trend that appeared to normally follow economic downturns (Sidener, 2009). The increase in second-career applicants presents opportunities for departments to expand their workforce to include individuals with prior experience in diverse careers, but the diversity does not end with these applicants' previous career choices. Individuals with prior careers outside law enforcement might present unique challenges by having differential training needs and abilities, previous work experience, levels of commitment, competing work values, familiarity with and attachment to wide varieties of perceived job benefits and rewards, and concepts of professionalism. Many of their attitudes toward work have been learned and ingrained through previous career experience, and organizations should be cautious in measuring the advantages and challenges of such candidates (COPS, 2009b).

The professional development of second-career police-officer candidates requires transferring previous career experience in a manner that suits both the department and the candidate's unique needs. In the field of education, a profession with many second-career applicants, several principles of learning guide the transfer of outside professional experience to new career paths. Extracting appropriate practical and professional expertise from previous career experience, adapting it to new work dimensions, and integrating these new employees into the organization to maximize their expertise, poses numerous challenges (Bolhuis, 2002; Tigchelaar, Brouwer, and Vermunt, 2010). Second-career applicants have different motivations and values, which can simultaneously invigorate and strain organizations unfamiliar with their special needs, and their levels of commitment might be used to organizational advantage (Pennington, Congdon, and Magilvy, 2007). In medicine, second-career applicants have been attractive because their life experiences and successes, as well as their perceived maturity, might enhance organizational mission with other applicants (Kohn and Truglio-Londrigan, 2007). Models of career transitions have described the potential effects of integrating second-career workers as mutually transformative, with organizations offering experienced persons previously unattainable potential for actualization in exchange for experience and maturity (Cary Cooper and Torrington, 1981; Bandow, Minsky, and Voss, 2007).

One solution to the complexities of hiring individuals with diverse previous experiences is to diagnose how their values fit with the organization. Schein's model of career anchors can be used to examine values and career priorities among workers from different fields and to assess their self-perceptions of talents, abilities, and values from prior experience (Danziger, Rachman-Moore, and Valency, 2008; Schein, 1990). For example, a second-career applicant with technical competence might struggle with service-oriented components of police work. An individual who seeks challenges might thrive on constant stimulation and not fit well in smaller agencies with limited opportunities. This model might help determine where training for second-career applicants should be focused. For example, for a former social worker appearing to be strong in public-service aspects of the job, training might best be focused on technical and tactical issues.

Supplying Candidates: Opening Up the "Faucet"

Some law-enforcement agencies have decided to "open the faucet" of supply by eliminating many traditional restrictions. Easing qualifications and hiring restrictions have often proved politically volatile and attracted criticism for being short-sighted (Maki, 2008; Spolar, 2009). For many agencies, the short-term concern for filling "empty chairs on test day" (Domash, 2002, p. 34) can be remedied by relaxing requirements. Yet, this leaves the challenge of finding qualified candidates while leading to charges that departments are lowering hiring standards.

Some agencies have sought to "open the faucet" by relaxing residency restrictions. This can negatively influence public perceptions of the police by leading to admission of applicants who have little knowledge of the communities they are to serve (DeMasi, 2003; Murphy and Worrall, 1999; Spolar, 2009). Some agencies have also eased educational requirements, rekindling debate about the desirability of degreed candidates as officers. Departments might also ease educational requirements to compensate for any exclusionary effect resulting from traditional barriers for minority and female applicants (Decker and Huckabee, 2002; White and Escobar, 2008). Some have relaxed minimum age requirements to attract more candidates, raising concern about the readiness of younger applicants for police work (Taylor et al., 2006). The Memphis (Tenn.) Police Department simultaneously lowered both its educational and residency requirements in 2007 and 2008 but has conducted no assessment of subsequent effect on recruitment (Maki, 2008). Some agencies have become more tolerant of experimental drug use, bad credit history, and minor arrest records to attain larger numbers of applicants (W. Lee, 2005; Taylor et al., 2006; Woska, 2006). Often, relaxing such restrictions interferes with the department's ability to build community confidence in the quality of its officers (Katz, 2000; Decker and Huckabee, 1999). At the same time, it can be seen as a rejection of the screening-out approach of candidate selection. Because of the potential organizational, political, and social ramifications of relaxed restrictions for departments and the communities they serve, before employing them, departments should carefully consider their effect on recruiting, as well as the signal they send about hiring standards.

Selecting Candidates

Often, the process of candidate selection becomes confused with the exercise of attracting applicants (Breaugh, 2008; Ellis et al., 2005). For the candidate, the selection process requires patient navigation of physical, mental, and aptitude screening examinations, interviews, and meetings and submitting to a thorough background investigation. The crucial task for agencies is to use selection methods that reveal the best possible recruits for department needs (Cavanagh, 2003; Scrivner, 2006).

Because screening and selection play pivotal roles in narrowing a large, generalized pool of interested persons to a manageable cohort of applicants, agencies often examine their selection procedures to ensure that the testing and screening process is consistent with what they seek in new officers (Searle, 2006). Efficiency, accuracy, and fairness are but a few of the concerns for departments in structuring this crucial task in the recruitment process. Yet, departments have changed their selection procedures very little since a 1973 review of police selection procedures by the National Advisory Committee on Criminal Justice Standards (Doerner, 1998; Langworthy, Hughes, and Sanders, 1995), even as departments seek to increase recruiting among women and minorities (Lim et al., 2009; J. Wilson and Grammich, 2009a).

Possible reasons for the relative stagnation of reforms of the selection process include the need for agencies to pattern their selection procedures after state mandates (Bradley, 2005), an overall practitioner attachment to more-reactive models of selection (Scrivner, 2006), and the difficulty in modifying a procedure without incentives to do so (Tuomey and Jolly, 2009). Community policing and generational differences have driven reexaminations of the selection process by forcing departments to rethink what specific characteristics they seek in their officers (DeCicco, 2000; Scrivner, 2006).

Although alternatives, such as the assessment center, to traditional hurdle approaches of selection have blossomed, evidence on them is mixed (DeCicco, 2000; Kolpack, 1991; Reuland and Stedman, 1998). Scores on assessment-center examinations are positively correlated with academy and patrol performance (Hogarty and Bromley, 1996; Dayan, Kasten, and Fox, 2002; Pynes and Bernardin, 1992) and supervisor performance (Ross, 1980) in preliminary empirical tests.

Nonetheless, when considering the challenge of recruiting qualified applicants from younger generations, departments should consider restructuring the process to account for both applicant perceptions and departmental goals. Applicants' top two reported frustrations about the selection process were the length of time and impersonality of the procedure, items that departments can correct (Switzer, 2006). Some agencies are also considering restructuring the order of selection tasks to ensure a diverse applicant pool and cut costs by eliminating unnecessary and redundant screening procedures (Haggerty, 2009). In structuring a departmental protocol for selecting the best candidates, departments should consider aligning selection procedures with what they consider to be important job dimensions (Scrivner, 2006). For example, if a department identifies residency as one of the most important job dimensions for applicants, screening for applicants' residence proximity would take place before that for most skills and abilities.

As selection procedures are subjected to closer scrutiny, predicting candidate success at various stages of the recruitment process (even in the training academy) has become increasingly important. The Las Vegas (Nev.) Police Department recently adopted a testing program designed to maximize department time and resources by processing only applicants who display a high probability (85 percent) of completing the process (J. Wilson and Grammich, 2009a). The LAPD has similarly streamlined its selection process to use predictive models (Lim et al., 2009). As agencies increasingly use predictive models, traditional hurdle approaches are slowly being infused with more–empirically based selection processes, especially for targeted populations of recruits.

Screening Processes. Since the early 1970s, the structure of police screening procedures has revolved around three basic tests: physical agility testing, psychological testing, and a medical examination (Ash, Slora, and Britton, 1990; Langworthy, Hughes, and Sanders, 1995). The exact prevalence of these screening procedures for police-candidate selection is unknown, but some studies indicate that they are used in about 90 percent of agencies (Ash, Slora, and Britton, 1990; DeCicco, 2000; Ho, 1999; Langworthy, Hughes, and Sanders, 1995). Yet, despite the dominant emphasis on these screening procedures, they have shown widely varying predictive value in determining success with a number of outcome measurements (White, 2008). Their chief effect is often to select out applicants from further consideration, meaning that tighter or more-rigorous selection processes will reduce the number of applicants.

Interview Procedures. Personal interviews are used in more than 95 percent of police agencies' selection efforts (Hickman and Reaves,

2006a). Interview processes are beginning to incorporate diverse stakeholders to examine for a broader "cultural fit" (J. Wilson and Grammich, 2009a), including values and beliefs consistent with department and community mission. Such interviews often take the form of an "oral board" protocol (Doerner, 1998). Some researchers have warned against relying heavily on oral-board interview techniques for reasons ranging from the lack of training for many interview board members to the use of ambiguous and invalid rating dimensions (Gaines and Kappeler, 1992). Nevertheless, some studies indicate that newer generations of recruits have been able to perform better on oral portions of the selection process than on written examinations, which might indicate the need for pretesting and access to practice written testing by computer (Whetstone, Reed, and Turner, 2006). The assessment-center approach has also been effective in yielding task-specific interview questions, shifting interview focus from standard question-and-answer format to interactive simulations and roleplay (Hogarty and Bromley, 1996; Dayan, Kasten, and Fox, 2002).

Background Investigations. Traditionally, background investigations and character references have formed the backbone of police selection techniques (Fulton, 2000; Langworthy, Hughes, and Sanders, 1995; Smelson, 1975). In early use, such studies correlated background problems with after-hire disciplinary issues (Cohen and Chaiken, 1972). Background investigations have proliferated in use as a screening tool, often being conducted at multiple stages by different levels of the organization (Ridgeway et al., 2008). The extent of these investigations in probing a candidate's background varies by locale and can often involve a lifetime criminal history check, a credit-bureau report, and examinations of close associates from the recent to the distant past (DeCicco, 2000; New York City Commission to Combat Police Corruption, 2008).

Younger generations pose unique challenges to such investigations. Applicants from these generations can be remarkably candid in disclosing personal information, but their impressions of what constitutes "character" might be startlingly different from those of evaluators (Russell, 2007; Verhoeven, Mashood, and Chansarkar, 2009). For instance, social-networking sites often display photographs of applicants in poses that older generations might think inappropriate. In the Internet age, conducting background investigations on candidates, especially those for whom computer use often constitutes a social reality, can be inherently problematic for law-enforcement agencies because of the sudden transparency with which younger generations are living their lives.[1] Similarly, financial background information on candidates might be of decreasing value in an era of increasing economic difficulties.

Recent research shows that biographical information gained from background investigations is of limited help in predicting subsequent officer termination (Brennan et al., 2009). As such, departments should proceed with caution and not place undue emphasis on a technique that appears to be steadily losing favor, especially for new generations of recruits, for whom transparency is assumed.

Predicting Future Success in Applicants

Closely related to the issue of electronic background investigation is electronic surveillance for the purposes of human-resource selection and its negative effect on recruiting as a whole. Recent research has indicated that a wealth of personal data about candidates can be obtained simply by searching the Internet for names, nicknames, email addresses, and addresses and looking at candidates' social-networking profiles (Searle, 2006). This power is increasing exponentially with the proliferation of electronic media and outpaces empirical study of its impact on recruitment efforts.

Yet, preliminary research shows that with such ability comes equal responsibility for the human-resource professional. Worries that such sensitive information might compromise individual freedom and privacy and adversely affect candidate selection have resonated with those concerned with civil liberties and organizational justice (Chapman and Webster, 2003; M. Harris, Van Hoye, and Lievens, 2003; Truxillo, Steiner, and Gilliland, 2004). The Internet age has changed the selection game

[1] Such transparency can also affect officers on the force. In one case, a Sandy Springs, Georgia, officer was fired for his Facebook postings, including one in which he divulged the possibility of a Federal Bureau of Investigation (FBI) drug seizure. See "Cop Says Facebook Postings Got Him Fired" (2009).

in ways that are still unclear for both job-seekers and agencies looking for qualified applicants.

What is apparent is that traditional methods of selection might be losing reliability in the absence of more-current data analysis on new generations of applicants and their changed career expectations, conflicting notions of privacy, and sustained cynicism about invasive and lengthy application processes. Placing these new recruits in uniform based on selection techniques that might not only be obsolete but also be seen as invasive and irrelevant could be counterproductive. Recent research demonstrating that personal demographic and background information (such as age, gender, and race) can predict police academy performance (White, 2008) appears not only to be contradicted by empiricists' inability to link academy performance to patrol behaviors but also to be in widespread disagreement about what qualities might best befit "good police officers" (Sanders, 2003). A more-proactive approach for selection would use department-specific benchmarks and performance measurements for determining what specific selection processes are a good fit for the department and keeping departmental needs assessments current for staffing.

Conclusion

Many of the core problems that police agencies face in recruiting have worsened in the past decade, even as changing economic conditions have led to temporary fluctuations in the numbers of recruits. Changing generational tastes for police work, increased prevalence of disqualifications (such as drug use or physical unfitness), and greater competition from other organizations (such as the military) have helped restrict the pool of qualified applicants. Further complicating recruiting efforts is the fragmented approach many agencies take to recruiting.

Nevertheless, agencies can take several modest steps to make their recruiting more effective. First, assessing their staffing needs can help shape a more-effective recruiting approach. This can include developing an assessment team, identifying budget and sources of revenue for recruiting, specifying organizational goals and values that recruits should have, and integrating the community in the hiring process.

Both internal and external strategies might help departments attract candidates. Internally, departments can build employee referral networks, create a recruitment unit, identify potential recruits from auxiliary or reserve ranks, and assess the effectiveness of their employee-engagement strategies (e.g., identify reasons employees should want to work for the agency). Externally, departments can use Internet and other electronic media, brand the department and its work within the community, use community liaisons to reach potential recruits, allow on-site visits, attend career and job fairs, and target both youth programs and second-career applicants. Such external marketing efforts should take care to ensure that agency work is portrayed realistically; portrayals of work that do not match the reality can cause the department to appear insincere in its efforts to engage.

Departments might also wish to expand their recruitment possibilities by opening wider the "faucet" of supply for recruits. Such efforts can include relaxing age, education, or residency requirements and becoming more tolerant of experimental drug use, bad credit history, or minor arrest records. Such initiatives, however, might raise concerns about the quality of recruits. Departments might also wish to expand their supply of candidates by revamping their screening processes, interview processes, and background investigations. At the same time, streamlined selection processes, particularly those aided by electronic media, should be cautious about applicant freedom and privacy, as well as about identifying characteristics of applicants likely to have success.

CHAPTER FIVE

The Most-Promising Practices for Maintaining Police Workforce Levels

In some ways, recruitment and retention are more of an art than a science. Empirical evidence on what appear to be promising practices is often lacking. Nevertheless, in concluding this work, we note several practices we have discussed that can affect multiple areas of recruitment and retention—and perhaps be of greatest promise to police agencies. Table 5.1 groups these practices into five categories, as presented earlier, and cites some relevant research on each. In this chapter, we also discuss the potential benefits and difficulties in them.

The benefits of *planning and analysis* can include understanding the depth and nature of the turnover problem. Gathering information on the problem might also identify issues that the organization can address to reduce turnover. The difficulty of planning and analysis lies in the organizational commitment required for it and to recognize the problem.

The benefits of *reducing the financial impact* of turnover include demonstrated long-term savings, as well as the opportunities the practices offer to dissolve myths about policing to applicants and to obtain a deeper understanding of the applicant pool. The difficulty of these practices is that they, too, require departmental resources. Offering realistic job previews, for example, can be labor intensive. Contracts might also conflict with generational career preferences and disrupt traditional relationships with employees.

The benefits of *enhancing compensation and other benefits* include their demonstrated effects on improving retention by meeting immediate employee needs, as well as its reinvigoration of the organization

Table 5.1
Practices and Relevant Research for Improving Police Recruitment and Retention

Practice	Relevant Research
Planning and analysis	
Analyze demographic trends, workload indicators, perceptions and attitudes toward law enforcement, and agency recruitment and retention patterns	
Survey officer job satisfaction and organizational commitment	J. Wilson and Grammich (2009a); Miller (2008); Orrick (2008a); Lim et al. (2009)
Conduct exit and stay interviews	
Identify and intervene with at-risk employees	
Reducing the financial impact	
Offer realistic job preview and extended ride-alongs	
Contracts with new employees	
Employ pretrained officers	Orrick (2008a); Kowal, Hassel, and Hassel (2008); Kickul (2002); Phillips (1998)
Provide apprentice salaries	
Use part-time staff	
Enhancing compensation and other benefits	
Increase and offer flexibility in compensation	
Give longevity pay increases	
Provide quality training and state-of-the-art equipment	
Offer tuition and relocation reimbursement	Prince (2003); Anderson and Gobeil (2003); Eaton (2003); Hill et al. (2001); Stanley (2008); Meier (1979); O'Brien-Pallas, Duffield, and Alksnis (2004)
Allow job flexibility and sharing	
Create alternative or compressed work schedules	
Provide multiple career ladders	
Offer other perks, such as on-site child care, fitness facilities, and take-home cars	

Employee engagement	
Implement practices to enhance compensation	Lloyd Morgan (undated); Cartwright and Holmes (2006); Towers Perrin (2003); Jamrog (2004); Butler and Felts (2006); Hegstad and Wentling (2004); Ingersoll and Smith (2003); Musser (2001); Smith and Ingersoll (2004)
Increase employee input in decisionmaking	
Offer evaluation and feedback opportunities	
Offer collaborative work and mentoring opportunities	
Offer job shadowing, rotating assignments, and cross-training	
Recognize exceptional work	
Improving organizational effectiveness	
Analyze recruitment and retention patterns	Lloyd Morgan (undated); Cartwright and Holmes (2006); Towers Perrin (2003); Jamrog (2004); Butler and Felts (2006); Hegstad and Wentling (2004); Ingersoll and Smith (2003); Musser (2001); Smith and Ingersoll (2004)
Survey job satisfaction	
Intervene with at-risk employees	
Conduct exit and stay interviews	
Improve hiring practices	
Pick the right supervisors and train them in management techniques	
Evaluate performance	
Eliminate unnecessary bureaucracy	
Fire unsuitable staff	
Improve communication	

through promotions. The potential difficulty of this strategy is the costs they impose, and the success that might vary, in part, by confidence recipients have in the longevity of such programs.

The benefits of *employee engagement* include demonstrated benefits of proper implementation for retention and the ties such practices can build between the employee and the agency, as well as between the agency and the community. The potential difficulty of this strategy is the need to implement more than symbolically and the potential costs in technology and restructuring of work.

The benefits of *improving organizational effectiveness* include better quality of supervision and leadership and improved training, which can help managers deal effectively with agency problems and even boost public perceptions of the department. The potential difficulty of this strategy is that it requires department commitment to developing better managerial staff. It requires sending managers for specialized training and might require an overhaul of the promotion process to appoint more-talented and more-capable individuals, as well as expensive potential changes in organization structure.

This guide does not address other key issues, such as specific ways of determining staffing need, allocation of staffing resources, distribution of staff attributes and qualities, and opportunity costs and implications that implementing recruiting and retention strategies has on other parts of the organization, which are also important to development of an effective, efficient workforce. Challenges might vary by agency and, especially, by local conditions confronting each agency.

The issues, and potential solutions we identify, will not apply to all agencies. Rather, our purpose was to provide a broad analysis of issues confronting many agencies and how these have developed over time. Each agency will face unique circumstances that it must consider in workforce planning.

Bibliography

Ahlrichs, Nancy S., *Competing for Talent: Key Recruitment and Retention Strategies for Becoming an Employer of Choice*, Palo Alto, Calif.: Davies-Black Publishing, 2000.

Alpert, Geoffrey P., "Hiring and Promoting Police Officers in Small Departments: The Role of Psychological Testing," *Criminal Law Bulletin*, Vol. 27, No. 3, May–June 1991, pp. 261–269.

Anderson, Madeleine, and Shalan Gobeil, *Recruitment and Retention in Child Welfare Services: A Survey of Child Welfare League of Canada Member Agencies*, Ottawa: Centre of Excellence for Child Welfare for Child Welfare League of Canada, 2003. As of May 21, 2010:
http://www.cwlc.ca/files/file/pubs/Recruitment%20in%20CW.pdf

Anderson, Neil, and Nicole Cunningham-Snell, "Personnel Selection," in Nik Chmiel, ed., *Introduction to Work and Organizational Psychology: A European Perspective*, Malden, Mass.: Blackwell Publishers, 2000, pp. 69–99.

Aronsson, Gunnar, "Influence of Worklife on Public Health," *Scandinavian Journal of Work, Environment and Health*, Vol. 25, No. 6, 1999, pp. 597–604. As of June 23, 2010:
http://www.sjweh.fi/show_abstract.php?abstract_id=486

Ash, Philip, Karen B. Slora, and Cynthia F. Britton, "Police Agency Officer Selection Practices," *Journal of Police Science and Administration*, Vol. 17, No. 4, December 1990, pp. 258–269.

Auten, James, "The Paramilitary Model of Police and Police Professionalism," *Policing: An International Journal of Police Strategies and Management*, Vol. 4, No. 67, 1981, pp. 67–72.

Avery, Derek R., and Patrick F. McKay, "Target Practice: An Organizational Impression Management Approach to Attracting Minority and Female Job Applicants," *Personnel Psychology*, Vol. 59, No. 1, Spring 2006, pp. 157–187.

Bacharach, Samuel B., Sharon Conley, and Joseph Shedd, "Beyond Career Ladders: Structuring Teacher Career Development Systems," *Teachers College Record*, Vol. 87, No. 4, Summer 1986, pp. 563–574.

Baker, Nicole, and Max Carrera, "Unlocking the Door to Relationship-Based Corrections Recruitment," *Corrections Today*, Vol. 69, No. 1, February 2007, pp. 36–38.

Bandow, Diane, Barbara D. Minsky, and Richard Steven Voss, "Reinventing the Future: Investigating Career Transitions from Industry to Academia," *Journal of Human Resources Education*, Vol. 1, No. 1, Summer 2007, pp. 23–37. As of June 23, 2010:
http://business.troy.edu/JHRE/Issue.aspx?Volume=1&Issue=1

Barber, Alison E., *Recruiting Employees: Individual and Organizational Perspectives*, Thousand Oaks, Calif.: Sage Publications, 1998.

Becker, Wendy S., and W. Mark Dale, "Strategic Human Resource Management in the Forensic Science Laboratory," *Forensic Science Communications*, Vol. 5, No. 4, October 2003, pp. 1–6. As of June 23, 2010:
http://www.fbi.gov/hq/lab/fsc/backissu/oct2003/2003_10_research01.htm

Best, Fred, *Work Sharing: The Issues, Policy Options, and Prospects*, Kalamazoo, Mich.: W. E. Upjohn Institute for Employment Research, 1981.

Birati, Assa, and Aharon Tziner, "Successful Promotion of Early Retirement: A Quantitative Approach," *Human Resource Management Review*, Vol. 5, No. 1, Spring 1995, pp. 53–62.

Bloomberg, Michael, "Mayor Mike Bloomberg Lays Out Plan for New York City Budget," *New York Daily News*, February 9, 2009. As of May 28, 2010:
http://www.nydailynews.com/opinions/2009/02/09/2009-02-09_mayor_mike_bloomberg_lays_out_plan_for_n.html

BLS—*See* Bureau of Labor Statistics.

Bolhuis, Sanneke, "Alternative Routes to Teaching in Secondary Education in the Netherlands," *European Journal of Teacher Education*, Vol. 25, No. 2–3, October 2002, pp. 223–238.

Bound, John, Michael Lovenheim, and Sarah E. Turner, *Understanding the Decrease in College Completion Rates and the Increased Time to the Baccalaureate Degree*, Ann Arbor, Mich.: University of Michigan Institute for Social Research, Population Studies Center research report 07-626, November 2007. As of June 23, 2010:
http://www.psc.isr.umich.edu/pubs/abs/4808

Bowyer, Richard F., *Recruiting 21st Century Army Warriors: A Task Requiring National Attention*, Carlisle Barracks, Pa.: U.S. Army War College, 2007. As of June 23, 2010:
http://handle.dtic.mil/100.2/ADA468428

Bradley, Patrick L., "21st Century Issues Related to Police Training and Standards," *Police Chief*, Vol. 72, No. 10, October 2005, pp. 32–39. As of June 23, 2010:
http://policechiefmagazine.org/magazine/index.cfm?fuseaction=display_arch&article_id=724&issue_id=102005

Brand, David, "The Future of Law Enforcement Recruiting: The Impact of Generation X," *Police Chief*, Vol. 8, August 1999, pp. 53–63.

Branham, Leigh, *The 7 Hidden Reasons Employees Leave: How to Recognize the Subtle Signs and Act Before It's Too Late*, Saratoga Springs, N.Y.: American Management Association, 2005.

Breaugh, James A., "Employee Recruitment: Current Knowledge and Important Areas for Further Research," *Human Resource Management Review*, Vol. 18, No. 3, September 2008, pp. 103–118.

Breaugh, James A., and Mary Starke, "Research on Employee Recruitment: So Many Studies, So Many Remaining Questions," *Journal of Management*, Vol. 26, No. 3, 2000, pp. 405–434.

Brennan, Adrianne M., Robert D. Davis, Cary D. Rostow, and Matrix Incorporated, "An Investigation of Biographical Information as Predictor of Employment Termination Among Law Enforcement Officers," *Journal of Police and Criminal Psychology*, Vol. 24, No. 2, October 2009, pp. 108–112.

Bureau of Labor Statistics, "Job Openings and Labor Turnover Survey," undated website. As of June 24, 2010:
http://www.bls.gov/jlt/

———, "May 2008 National Occupational Employment and Wage Estimates, United States," *Occupational Employment Statistics*, last modified May 29, 2009. As of June 24, 2010:
http://www.bls.gov/oes/2008/may/oes_nat.htm

Butler, Martha R., and Joan Felts, "Tool Kit for the Staff Mentor: Strategies for Improving Retention," *Journal of Continuing Education in Nursing*, Vol. 37, No. 5, September–October 2006, pp. 210–213.

Butterfield, Fox, "Urban Police Jobs Are Losing Their Appeal," *New York Times*, July 30, 2001. As of June 23, 2010:
http://www.nytimes.com/2001/07/30/national/30POLI.html

Buzawa, Eva Schlesinger, *The Role of Selected Factors upon Patrol Officer Job Satisfaction in Two Urban Police Departments*, East Lansing, Mich.: Michigan State University, Ph.D. dissertation, 1979.

———, "Determining Patrol Officer Job Satisfaction: The Role of Selected Demographic and Job-Specific Attitudes," *Criminology*, Vol. 22, No. 1, February 1984, pp. 61–81.

Buzawa, Eva Schlesinger, Thomas L. Austin, and James Bannon, "The Role of Selected Socio-Demographics and Job-Specific Variables in Predicting Patrol Officer Job Satisfaction: A Reexamination Ten Years Later," *American Journal of Police*, Vol. 13, No. 2, 1994, pp. 51–75.

Byrne, John, "Prospect Heights Police Are on Duty, but Station Shut to Public," *Chicago Tribune*, July 10, 2009. As of June 23, 2010:
http://articles.chicagotribune.com/2009-07-10/news/0907090887_1_police-officers-shut-furloughs

Byrne, Roger, "Employees: Capital or Commodity?" *Learning Organization*, Vol. 8, No. 1, 2001, pp. 44–50.

Cable, Daniel M., and Kang Yang Trevor Yu, "Managing Job Seekers' Organizational Image Beliefs: The Role of Media Richness and Media Credibility," *Journal of Applied Psychology*, Vol. 91, No. 4, July 2006, pp. 828–840.

California Commission on Peace Officer Standards and Training, *POST Recruitment Strategic Planning Guide: Finding and Keeping the Right People*, Sacramento, Calif.: California POST Media Distribution, November 2009. As of June 23, 2010:
http://lib.post.ca.gov/Publications/RecruitmentStrategicPlanningGuide_11-09.pdf

California Police Chiefs Association, "Demographic Survey, 1994," Sacramento, Calif., 1994.

———, "Demographic Survey, 2001," Sacramento, Calif., 2001.

———, "Demographic Survey, 2004," Sacramento, Calif., November 2004. As of June 23, 2010:
http://www.californiapolicechiefs.org/nav_files/research/pdfs/04demosurvey.pdf

Camper, John, and Rick Brown, "'Déjà Vu All Over Again': Meeting the Challenges of Funding Cuts in Patrol Operations," *PERF Subject to Debate*, Vol. 22, No. 12, December 2008, pp. 1–6. As of June 23, 2010:
http://www.coronasolutions.com/downloads/perf.pdf

Canadian Association of Chiefs of Police, Canadian Police Association, PricewaterhouseCoopers, and Human Resources Development Canada, *Strategic Human Resources Analysis of Public Policing in Canada*, Ottawa: PricewaterhouseCoopers, 2000.

Cangelosi, Joseph D., F. Scott Markham, and William T. Bounds, "Factors Related to Nurse Retention and Turnover: An Updated Study," *Health Marketing Quarterly*, Vol. 15, No. 3, June 1998, pp. 25–43.

Cantor, Jeffrey A., "Registered Pre-Apprenticeship: Successful Practices Linking School to Work," *Journal of Industrial Teacher Education*, Vol. 34, No. 3, Spring 1997, pp. 35–58.

Carter, David L., and Allen D. Sapp, "College Education and Policing: Coming of Age," *FBI Law Enforcement Bulletin*, Vol. 61, No. 1, January 1992, pp. 8–14.

Cartwright, Susan, and Nicola Holmes, "The Meaning of Work: The Challenge of Regaining Employee Engagement and Reducing Cynicism," *Human Resource Management Review*, Vol. 16, No. 2, June 2006, pp. 199–208.

Castro, Hector, "Bad Economy Good for Police Recruiting," *Seattle Post-Intelligencer*, October 2, 2009. As of June 23, 2010:
http://www.seattlepi.com/local/410721_cops02.html

Cavanagh, Michael E., *Policing Within a Professional Framework*, Upper Saddle River, N.J.: Pearson Prentice Hall, 2003.

Chambers, Brad A., "Applicant Reactions and Their Consequences: Review, Advice, and Recommendations for Future Research," *International Journal of Management Reviews*, Vol. 4, No. 4, December 2002, pp. 317–333.

Chambers, Stanley B., "Police Work Looks Good to Many," *Raleigh News and Observer*, May 5, 2009. As of June 23, 2010:
http://www.newsobserver.com/2009/05/05/56274/police-work-looks-good-to-many.html

Chapman, Derek S., and Jane Webster, "The Use of Technologies in the Recruitment, Screening, and Selection Processes for Job Candidates," *International Journal of Selection and Assessment*, Vol. 11, No. 2–3, June 2003, pp. 113–120.

Charrier, Kim, "Marketing Strategies for Attracting and Retaining Generation X Police Officers," *Police Chief*, Vol. 67, No. 12, December 2000, pp. 45–51.

Chien, Chen-Fu, and Li-Fei Chen, "Data Mining to Improve Personnel Selection and Enhance Human Capital: A Case Study in High-Technology Industry," *Expert Systems with Applications*, Vol. 34, No. 1, January 2008, pp. 280–290.

City of Houston, Police Department, "HPD Careers," undated Web page. As of July 2, 2010:
http://www.houstontx.gov/police/careers.htm

Clem, Connie, Barbara Krauth, and Paula Wenger, *Recruitment, Hiring, and Retention: Current Practices in U.S. Jails*, Longmont, Colo.: National Institute of Corrections Information Center, 2000. As of June 23, 2010:
http://nicic.gov/Library/015885

Codispoti, Amanda, "Many Apply for Police Job Slots," *Roanoke Times*, March 11, 2009. As of June 23, 2010:
http://www.roanoke.com/news/roanoke/wb/197315

Cohen, Bernard, and Jan M. Chaiken, *Police Background Characteristics and Performance: Summary*, Santa Monica, Calif.: RAND Corporation, R-999/1-DOJ, 1972. As of June 23, 2010:
http://www.rand.org/pubs/reports/R999.1/

Cohen-Charash, Yochi, and Paul E. Spector, "The Role of Justice in Organizations: A Meta-Analysis," *Organizational Behavior and Human Decision Processes*, Vol. 86, No. 2, November 2001, pp. 278–321.

Cooper, Cary L., and Derek Torrington, eds., *After Forty: The Time for Achievement?* New York: Wiley, 1981.

Cooper, Christine, and Samantha Ingram, "*Retaining Officers in the Police Service: A Study of Resignations and Transfers in Ten Forces*, London: Home Office Research, Development and Statistics Directorate, NCJ 205347, 2004. As of June 23, 2010:
http://www.homeoffice.gov.uk/rds/pdfs04/r212.pdf

"Cop Says Facebook Postings Got Him Fired," *WSBTV.com*, December 8, 2009. As of June 23, 2010:
http://www.wsbtv.com/news/21900267/detail.html

Copeland, Thomas N., "Officer Retention: The Next Leadership Challenge," *Criminal Justice Institute Management Quarterly*, Winter 2009. As of June 23, 2010: http://www.cji.edu/Files/MQ2009Winter.pdf

COPS—*See* U.S. Department of Justice, Office of Community Oriented Policing Services.

Crowe, Robert, "Economy Has Folks Feeling the Blue," *San Antonio Express-News,* February 8, 2009. As of June 23, 2010: http://www.mysanantonio.com/news/local_news/Economy_has_folks_feeling_the_blue.html

Cunningham, Sonia, and Melissa Wagstaff, *Reflecting London: Diversity of Police Community Support Officer Recruits Compared to Police Officer Recruits in the Metropolitan Police Service*, London: Metropolitan Police Authority, December 2006. As of June 23, 2010: http://www.mpa.gov.uk/downloads/publications/pcso-diversity-full.pdf

Currier, Joel, "Missouri Police Academies Grow Despite Budget Tightening," *St. Louis Post-Dispatch,* November 2, 2009. As of June 23, 2010: http://www.columbiamissourian.com/stories/2009/11/09/mo-police-academies-seeing-growth/

Dantzker, Mark L., "Designing a Measure of Job Satisfaction for Policing: A Research Note," *Journal of Crime and Justice*, Vol. 16, No. 2, 1993, pp. 171–181.

———, "Measuring Job Satisfaction in Police Departments and Policy Implications: An Examination of a Mid-Size, Southern Police Department," *American Journal of Police*, Vol. 13, No. 2, 1994, pp. 77–101.

Danziger, Nira, Dalia Rachman-Moore, and Rony Valency, "The Construct Validity of Schein's Career Anchors Orientation Inventory," *Career Development International*, Vol. 13, No. 1, 2008, pp. 7–19.

Davenport, Thomas H., Robert J. Thomas, and Susan Cantrell, "The Mysterious Art and Science of Knowledge-Worker Performance," *MIT Sloan Management Review*, Vol. 44, No. 1, Fall 2002, pp. 23–30.

Davis, Lois M., Louis T. Mariano, Jennifer E. Pace, Sarah K. Cotton, and Paul Steinberg, *Combating Terrorism: How Prepared Are State and Local Response Organizations?* Santa Monica, Calif.: RAND Corporation, MG-309-OSD, 2006. As of June 24, 2010: http://www.rand.org/pubs/monographs/MG309/

Dayan, Kobi, Ronen Kasten, and Shaul Fox, "Entry-Level Police Candidate Assessment Center: An Efficient Tool or a Hammer to Kill a Fly?" *Personnel Psychology*, Vol. 55, No. 4, January 2002, pp. 827–849.

DeCicco, David A., "Police Officer Candidate Assessment and Selection," *FBI Law Enforcement Bulletin*, Vol. 69, No. 12, December 2000, pp. 1–6.

Decker, Lisa Kay, and Robert G. Huckabee, "Law Enforcement Hiring Practices and Narrowing the Applicant Pool: A Case Study," *Journal of Offender Rehabilitation*, Vol. 29, No. 3–4, December 1999, pp. 57–70.

———, "Raising the Age and Education Requirements for Police Officers: Will Too Many Women and Minority Candidates Be Excluded?" *Policing: An International Journal of Police Strategies and Management*, Vol. 25, No. 4, 2002, pp. 789–802.

Delaware State Personnel Office, "Research Project: Phase 1," Newark, Del.: University of Delaware, Institute for Public Administration, June 2002.

Del Bueno, Dorothy J., "Reflections on Retention, Recognition, and Rewards," *Journal of Nursing Administration*, Vol. 23, No. 10, October 1993, pp. 6–7, 41.

DeLord, Ron, special counsel to the executive director, Combined Law Enforcement Associations of Texas, interview, "From the Field Experiences," Santa Monica, Calif.: RAND Corporation, June 2009. As of June 24, 2010: http://www.rand.org/ise/centers/quality_policing/cops/resources/field_experiences/ron_delord.html

DeMasi, Michael, "Change in Residency Rule Sought: Police Officials Say Law Hurts Recruitment," *Schenectady Daily Gazette*, August 19, 2003.

Derby, Wade J., "The Impact of Drug Decriminalization on the Future of Police Recruiting Standards," *Police Chief*, Vol. 75, No. 8, August 2008, pp. 92–95.

De Rugy, Veronique, "Facts and Figures About Homeland Security Spending," Washington, D.C.: American Enterprise Institute, December 14, 2006. As of June 24, 2010:
http://www.aei.org/docLib/20061214_FactsandFigures.pdf

Dick, Penny, "The Social Construction of the Meaning of Acute Stressors: A Qualitative Study of the Personal Accounts of Police Officers Using a Stress Counselling Service," *Work and Stress*, Vol. 14, No. 3, July 2000, pp. 226–244.

Dobbins, James, John G. McGinn, Keith Crane, Seth G. Jones, Rollie Lal, Andrew Rathmell, Rachel M. Swanger, and Anga R. Timilsina, *America's Role in Nation-Building: From Germany to Iraq*, Santa Monica, Calif.: RAND Corporation, MR-1753-RC, 2003. As of June 24, 2010:
http://www.rand.org/pubs/monograph_reports/MR1753/

DoD—*See* U.S. Department of Defense.

Doerner, William G., "Officer Retention Patterns: An Affirmative Action Concern for Police Agencies?" *American Journal of Police*, Vol. 14, No. 3–4, 1995, pp. 197–210.

———, *Introduction to Law Enforcement: An Insider's View*, Boston, Mass.: Butterworth-Heinemann, 1998.

Domash, Shelley F., "Who Wants This Job?" *Police*, Vol. 26, No. 5, May 2002, pp. 34–39.

Donnelly, Daniel, "Policing the Scottish Community," in Daniel Donnelly and Kenneth Scott, eds., *Policing Scotland*, Cullompton, Devon, U.K.: Willan Publishing, 2005, pp. 130–156.

Draut, Tamara, *Economic State of Young America*, New York: Demos, 2008. As of June 24, 2010:
http://www.demos.org/pubs/esya_web.pdf

Draut, Tamara, and Javier Silva, *Generation Broke: The Growth of Debt Among Young Americans*, New York: Demos, briefing paper 2, October 2004. As of June 24, 2010:
http://archive.demos.org/pubs/Generation_Broke.pdf

Drew, Jacqueline, Sally A. Carless, and Briony M. Thompson, "Predicting Turnover of Police Officers Using the Sixteen Personality Factor Questionnaire," *Journal of Criminal Justice*, Vol. 36, No. 4, August 2008, pp. 326–331.

Dupont, Benoît, *Preserving Institutional Memory in Australian Police Services*, Canberra: Australian Institute of Criminology, Trends and Issues in Crime and Criminal Justice 245, 2003.

Dynarski, Susan M., *Building the Stock of College-Educated Labor*, Cambridge, Mass.: National Bureau of Economic Research, working paper 11604, August 2005. As of June 24, 2010:
http://www.nber.org/papers/W11604.pdf

Eaton, Susan C., "If You Can Use Them: Flexibility Policies, Organizational Commitment, and Perceived Performance," *Industrial Relations*, Vol. 42, No. 2, 2003, pp. 145–167.

Edmonton police official, personal communication, October 5, 2009.

Edwards, Gary Scott, *Generational Competence and Retention: A Study of Different Generations in Law Enforcement and How These Differences Impact Retention in the Chesterfield County Police Department*, Richmond, Va.: University of Richmond, thesis, 2007.

Egan, Timothy, "Police Forces, Their Ranks Thin, Offer Bonuses, Bounties and More," *New York Times*, December 28, 2005. As of June 24, 2010:
http://www.nytimes.com/2005/12/28/national/28police.html

Ellis, Gene, Greg Marshall, Chris Skinner, and Gary Smith, "Using Visual Technology for Recruitment," *Police Chief*, Vol. 72, No. 1, January 2005, pp. 20–24.

Ensher, Ellen A., and Susan E. Murphy, "Effects of Race, Gender, Perceived Similarity, and Contact on Mentor Relationships," *Journal of Vocational Behavior*, Vol. 50, No. 3, June 1997, pp. 460–481.

Enz, Cathy A., and Judy A. Siguaw, "Best Practices in Human Resources," *Cornell Hotel and Restaurant Administration Quarterly*, Vol. 41, No. 1, February 2000, pp. 48–61.

Eskildsen, Jacob K., and Mikkel L. Nussler, "The Managerial Drivers of Employee Satisfaction and Loyalty," *Total Quality Management and Business Excellence*, Vol. 11, No. 4–6, July 2000, pp. 581–588.

"Even Cops Losing Their Jobs in Recession," Associated Press, June 24, 2009.

Faher, Mike, "City Police Filling Holes in Ranks," *Johnstown Tribune-Democrat*, June 13, 2009. As of June 24, 2010:
http://tribune-democrat.com/local/x519194658/City-police-filling-holes-in-ranks

FBI—*See* Federal Bureau of Investigation.

Federal Bureau of Investigation, "The Cyber Threat Today: Major Attacks on the Rise," October 17, 2008. As of June 24, 2010:
http://www.fbi.gov/page2/oct08/cyberthreat101708.html

———, "Crime in the United States: Preliminary Annual Uniform Crime Report, January to December 2008," June 1, 2009. As of June 24, 2010:
http://www.fbi.gov/ucr/08aprelim/index.html

Fielding, N. G., and J. L. Fielding, "Study of Resignation During British Police Training," *Journal of Police Science and Administration*, Vol. 15, No. 1, March 1987, pp. 24–36.

Fischer, Craig, *Violent Crime and the Economic Crisis: Police Chiefs Face a New Challenge*, Washington, D.C.: Police Executive Research Forum, May 2009.

Fischer, Margaret A., *Best Practices Guide for Generation X Recruits and the Field Training Experience*, Gaithersburg, Md.: International Association of Chiefs of Police, 2006. As of June 24, 2010:
http://www.theiacp.org/Portals/0/pdfs/Publications/BP-GenXRecruits.pdf

Fitzgerald, Joan, "The Potential and Limitations of Career Ladders," in Joan Fitzgerald, *Moving Up in the New Economy: Career Ladders for U.S. Workers*, Ithaca, N.Y.: Cornell University Press, 2006, pp. 1–23.

Flood, Patrick C., Thomas Turner, Nagarajan Ramamoorthy, and Jill Pearson, "Causes and Consequences of Psychological Contracts Among Knowledge Workers in the High Technology and Financial Services Industries," *International Journal of Human Resource Management*, Vol. 12, No. 7, November 2001, pp. 1152–1165.

Flynn, Kevin, "As Opportunity Knocks, Police Turn in Badges," *New York Times*, August 12, 2000. As of June 24, 2010:
http://www.nytimes.com/2000/08/12/nyregion/as-opportunity-knocks-police-turn-in-badges.html

Folger, Robert, and Mary A. Konovsky, "Effects of Procedural and Distributive Justice on Reactions to Pay Raise Decisions," *Academy of Management Journal*, Vol. 32, No. 1, March 1989, pp. 115–130.

Fox, Patrick, "Proposed Police Cuts Anger Gwinnett Residents," *Atlanta Journal-Constitution*, July 20, 2009. As of June 24, 2010:
http://www.ajc.com/news/gwinnett/proposed-police-cuts-anger-96246.html

Frawley, Kathleen E., *The Effects of 9/11 on the Fire Fighter Labor Market*, Bloomington, Ill.: Illinois Wesleyan University, Economics Department Honors Projects paper 7, 2006. As of June 24, 2010:
http://digitalcommons.iwu.edu/econ_honproj/7/

Friedman, Raymond A., and Brooks Holtom, "The Effects of Network Groups on Minority Employee Turnover Intentions," *Human Resource Management*, Vol. 41, No. 4, Winter 2002, pp. 405–421.

Fritsch, Eric J., John Liederbach, and Robert W. Taylor, *Police Patrol Allocation and Deployment*, Upper Saddle River, N.J.: Pearson Prentice Hall, 2009.

Frost, Jeffrey A., *Predictors of Job Satisfaction and Turnover Intention in Police Organizations: A Procedural Approach*, Chicago, Ill.: University of Chicago, Ph.D. dissertation, 2006.

Fry, Louise W., and Leslie J. Berkes, "Paramilitary Police Model: An Organizational Misfit," *Human Organization*, Vol. 42, No. 3, Fall 1983, pp. 225–234.

Fulton, Roger, "Recruiting and Hiring New Officers," *Law Enforcement Technology*, Vol. 30, August 2000, p. 130.

Fyfe, James J., Jack R. Greene, William F. Walsh, O. W. Wilson, and Roy Clinton McLaren, eds., *Police Administration*, 5th ed., New York: McGraw-Hill, 1997.

Gaines, Larry K., and Victor E. Kappeler, "Selection and Testing," in Gary W. Cordner and Donna C. Hale, eds., *What Works in Policing? Operations and Administration Examined*, Cincinnati, Ohio: Anderson Publishing, 1992, pp. 107–123.

Geis, Gilbert, and Elvin Cavanagh, "Recruitment and Retention of Correctional Personnel," *Crime and Delinquency*, Vol. 12, No. 3, July 1966, pp. 232–239.

Gettinger, Stephen H., *Assessing Criminal Justice Needs*, Washington, D.C.: U.S. Department of Justice, National Institute of Justice, June 1984.

Glanville, Kathleen, "Portland Police Recruits Hit the Streets Earlier," *Oregonian*, July 11, 2009. As of June 24, 2010:
http://www.oregonlive.com/portland/index.ssf/2009/07/portland_police_recruits_hit_t.html

Goeller, Annie, "Economy Leads to Surge in Applications for Government Jobs in Johnson County," *Indiana Economic Digest*, June 29, 2009. As of June 24, 2010:
http://www.indianaeconomicdigest.net/main.asp?SectionID=31&ArticleID=48559

Goldstein, Herman, *Policing a Free Society*, Cambridge, Mass.: Ballinger Publishing, 1977.

Golfin, Peggy A., *A Proposed Pilot to Recruit Pretrained Personnel*, Alexandria, Va.: CNA Corporation, January 2006.

Gottfredson, Michael R., and Don M. Gottfredson, *Decision Making in Criminal Justice: Toward the Rational Exercise of Discretion*, 2nd ed., New York: Plenum Press, 1988.

Graig, Laurene, and Valerie Paganelli, "Phased Retirement: Reshaping the End of Work," *Compensation and Benefits Management*, Vol. 16, No. 2, Spring 2000, pp. 1–9.

Greene, Maureen T., and Mary S. Puetzer, "The Value of Mentoring: A Strategic Approach to Retention and Recruitment," *Journal of Nursing Care Quality*, Vol. 17, No. 1, October 2002, pp. 63–70.

Griffin, Gerald R., Roger L. Dunbar, and Michael E. McGill, "Factors Associated with Job Satisfaction Among Police Personnel," *Journal of Police Science and Administration*, Vol. 6, No. 1, March 1978, pp. 77–85.

Gubbins, M. Claire, and Thomas N. Garavan, "The Changing Context and Role of the HRD Professional: Time to Recognize the Importance of Social Networking Competency," paper presented at the Ninth Annual Conference on Human Resource Development, Lille, France, May 2008.

Gunnels-Perry, Sherryl, "Public/Private Partnerships as Recruiting and Retention Strategies," *Employment Relations Today*, Vol. 26, No. 2, January 2007, pp. 1–13.

Haarr, Robin N., "Factors Affecting the Decision of Police Recruits to 'Drop Out' of Police Work," *Police Quarterly*, Vol. 8, No. 4, December 2005, pp. 431–453.

Haggerty, Catherine, lieutenant, recruiting division, Austin Police Department, interview, "From the Field Experiences," Santa Monica, Calif.: RAND Corporation, July 2009. As of June 24, 2010:
http://www.rand.org/ise/centers/quality_policing/cops/resources/field_experiences/catherine_haggerty.html

Harrington, Penny E., *Recruiting and Retaining Women: A Self-Assessment Guide for Law Enforcement*, Los Angeles, Calif.: National Center for Women and Policing, a Division of the Feminist Majority Foundation, 2000. As of June 24, 2010:
http://www.ncjrs.gov/pdffiles1/bja/185235.pdf

Harris, Louis M., and J. Norman Baldwin, "Voluntary Turnover of Field Operations Officers: A Test of Confluency Theory," *Journal of Criminal Justice*, Vol. 27, No. 6, November–December 1999, pp. 483–493.

Harris, Michael M., Greet Van Hoye, and Filip Lievens, "Privacy and Attitudes Towards Internet-Based Selection Systems: A Cross-Cultural Comparison," *International Journal of Selection and Assessment*, Vol. 11, No. 2–3, June 2003, pp. 230–236.

Harrison, Bob, "Gamers, Millennials, and Generation Next: Implications for Policing," *Police Chief*, Vol. 74, No. 10, October 2007, pp. 150–160.

Hausknecht, John, Julianne M. Rodda, and Michael J. Howard, *Targeted Employee Retention: Performance-Based and Job-Related Differences in Reported Reasons for Staying*, Ithaca, N.Y.: Cornell University School of Industrial and Labor Relations, April 2008. As of June 24, 2010:
http://digitalcommons.ilr.cornell.edu/articles/140/

Hazucha, Joy F., Sarah A. Hezlett, and Robert J. Schneider, "The Impact of 360-Degree Feedback on Management Skills Development," *Human Resource Management*, Vol. 32, No. 2–3, Summer 1993, pp. 325–352.

Hegstad, Christine D., and Rose Mary Wentling, "The Development and Maintenance of Exemplary Formal Mentoring Programs in Fortune 500 Companies," *Human Resource Development Quarterly*, Vol. 15, No. 4, Winter 2004, pp. 421–448.

Herman, Roger E., "HR Managers as Employee-Retention Specialists," *Employee Relations Today*, Vol. 32, No. 2, July 2005, pp. 1–7.

Hickman, Matthew J., "Impact of the Military Reserve Activation on Police Staffing," *Police Chief*, Vol. 73, No. 10, October 2006, pp. 12–14.

Hickman, Matthew J., and Brian A. Reaves, *Local Police Departments, 2003*, Washington, D.C.: Department of Justice, Office of Justice Programs, Bureau of Justice Statistics, NCJ 210118, April 1, 2006a. As of June 24, 2010:
http://bjs.ojp.usdoj.gov/index.cfm?ty=pbdetail&iid=1045

———, *Sheriffs' Offices, 2003*, Washington, D.C.: Department of Justice, Office of Justice Programs, Bureau of Justice Statistics, NCJ 211361, April 1, 2006b. As of June 24, 2010:
http://bjs.ojp.usdoj.gov/index.cfm?ty=pbdetail&iid=1217

Hill, E. Jeffrey, Alan J. Hawkins, Maria Ferris, and Michelle Weitzman, "Finding an Extra Day a Week: The Positive Influence of Perceived Job Flexibility on Work and Family," *Family Relations*, Vol. 50, No. 1, January 2001, pp. 49–58.

Ho, Taiping, "Assessment of Police Officer Recruiting and Testing Instruments," *Journal of Offender Rehabilitation*, Vol. 29, No. 3–4, December 1999, pp. 1–23.

Hoffman, J., "Plague of Small Agencies: Turnover," *Law and Order*, Vol. 41, No. 6, June 1993, pp. 25–28.

Hogarty, Kris, and Max Bromley, "Evaluating the Use of the Assessment Center Process for Entry-Level Police Officer Selections in a Medium Sized Police Agency," *Journal of Police and Criminal Psychology*, Vol. 11, No. 1, March 1996, pp. 27–34.

Hogue, Mark C., Tommie Black, and Robert T. Sigler, "Differential Use of Screening Techniques in the Recruitment of Police Officers," *American Journal of Police*, Vol. 13, No. 2, 1994, pp. 113–124.

Holtom, Brooks C., Terence R. Mitchell, and Thomas W. Lee, "Increasing Human and Social Capital by Applying Job Embeddedness Theory," *Organizational Dynamics*, Vol. 35, No. 4, 2006, pp. 316–331.

Holtom, Brooks C., Terence R. Mitchell, Thomas W. Lee, and Marion B. Eberly, "Turnover and Retention Research: A Glance at the Past, a Closer Review of the Present, and a Venture into the Future," *Academy of Management Annals*, Vol. 2, No. 1, August 2008, pp. 231–274.

Hom, Peter W., *Turnover Costs Among Mental Health Professionals*, Tempe, Ariz.: College of Business, Arizona State University, Ph.D. dissertation, 1992.

Hom, Peter W., and Rodger W. Griffeth, *Employee Turnover*, Cincinnati, Ohio: South-Western College Publishing, 1994.

Hurst, Susan, and Stephanie Koplin-Baucum, "Role Acquisition, Socialization, and Retention: Unique Aspects of a Mentoring Program," *Journal for Nurses in Staff Development*, Vol. 19, No. 4, July–August 2003, pp. 176–180.

IACP—*See* International Association of Chiefs of Police.

Idaho State Police, "Realistic Job Preview," undated Web page. As of June 24, 2010: http://www.isp.idaho.gov/hr/trooper_info/realistic_job.html

Ingersoll, Richard M., and Thomas M. Smith, "The Wrong Solution to the Teacher Shortage," *Educational Leadership*, Vol. 60, No. 8, May 2003, pp. 30–33.

International Association of Chiefs of Police, "Discover Policing," undated website. As of June 24, 2010:
http://discoverpolicing.org/

International Association of Directors of Law Enforcement Standards and Training, *Reciprocity Handbook*, Meridian, Ida., 2005.

Jackson, Jodie, C. Ken Shannon, Donald E. Pathman, Elaine Mason, and James W. Nemitz, "A Comparative Assessment of West Virginia's Financial Incentive Programs for Rural Physicians," *Journal of Rural Health*, Vol. 19, No. 5, 2003, pp. 329–339.

Jamrog, Jay, "The Perfect Storm: The Future of Retention and Engagement," *Human Resource Planning*, Vol. 27, No. 3, 2004, pp. 26–33.

Jaramillo, Fernando, Robert Nixon, and Doreen Sams, "The Effect of Law Enforcement Stress on Organizational Commitment," *Policing: An International Journal of Police Strategies and Management,* Vol. 28, No. 2, 2005, pp. 321-336.

Johnson, Kevin, "Economy Forces Deep Police Cuts," *Arizona Republic*, October 19, 2008. As of June 24, 2010:
http://www.azcentral.com/news/articles/2008/10/19/20081019crime-economy1019.html

Johnston, Lloyd D., Patrick M. O'Malley, Jerald G. Bachman, and John E. Schulenberg, "Various Stimulant Drugs Show Continuing Gradual Declines Among Teens in 2008, Most Illicit Drugs Hold Steady," press release, Ann Arbor, Mich.: University of Michigan News Service, December 11, 2008. As of June 24, 2010:
http://monitoringthefuture.org/data/08data.html#2008data-drugs

Jones, Seth G., Jeremy M. Wilson, Andrew Rathmell, and K. Jack Riley, *Establishing Law and Order After Conflict*, Santa Monica, Calif.: RAND Corporation, MG-374-RC, 2005. As of June 24, 2010:
http://www.rand.org/pubs/monographs/MG374/

Jordan, William T., Lorie Fridell, Donald Faggiani, and Bruce Kubu, "Attracting Females and Racial/Ethnic Minorities to Law Enforcement," *Journal of Criminal Justice*, Vol. 37, No. 4, July–August 2009, pp. 333–341.

Kacmar, K. Michele, Martha C. Andrews, David L. Van Rooy, R. Chris Steilberg, and Stephen Cerrone, "Sure Everyone Can Be Replaced . . . but at What Cost? Turnover as a Predictor of Unit-Level Performance," *Academy of Management Journal*, Vol. 49, No. 1, February 2006, pp. 133–144.

Kahanov, Leamor, and Lanna Andrews, "A Survey of Athletic Training Employers' Hiring Criteria," *Journal of Athletic Training*, Vol. 36, No. 4, October–December 2001, pp. 408–412.

Kane, Tim, "The Demographics of Military Enlistment After 9/11," Washington, D.C.: Heritage Foundation, executive memorandum 987, November 3, 2005. As of June 24, 2010:
http://www.heritage.org/Research/Reports/2005/11/The-Demographics-of-Military-Enlistment-After-9-11

Kappeler, Victor E., Richard D. Sluder, and Geoffrey P. Alpert, *Forces of Deviance: Understanding the Dark Side of Policing*, Prospect Heights, Ill.: Waveland Press, 1994.

Katz, Jesse, "Past Drug Use, Future Cops," *Los Angeles Times*, June 18, 2000. As of June 24, 2010:
http://articles.latimes.com/2000/jun/18/news/mn-42251

Kearns, Scott Alan, *Recruitment and Retention Challenges for Law Enforcement Agencies: Identifying the Reasons for High Turnover Rates of New Recruits*, Richmond, Va.: University of Richmond, thesis, 2007.

Khashu, Anita, and Mary Malina, *The Role of Local Police: Striking a Balance Between Immigration Enforcement and Civil Liberties*, Washington, D.C.: Police Foundation, April 2009. As of June 24, 2010:
http://www.policefoundation.org/pdf/strikingabalance/Narrative.pdf

Kickul, Jill, "Promises Made, Promises Broken: An Exploration of Employee Attraction and Retention Practices in Small Business," *Journal of Small Business Management*, Vol. 39, No. 4, 2002, pp. 320–335.

Kim, Soonhee, "Factors Affecting State Government Information Technology Employee Turnover Intentions," *American Review of Public Administration*, Vol. 35, No. 2, 2005, pp. 137–156.

Kirpal, Simone, "Work Identities of Nurses: Between Caring and Efficiency Demands," *Career Development International*, Vol. 9, No. 3, 2004, pp. 274–304.

Kogi, Kazutaka, "Implications of Flexible Work Systems for Work Studies," *Journal of Human Ergology*, Vol. 26, No. 2, December 1997, pp. 89–97.

Kohn, Paula S., and Marie Truglio-Londrigan, "Second-Career Baccalaureate Nursing Students: A Lived Experience," *Journal of Nursing Education*, Vol. 46, No. 9, September 2007, pp. 391–399.

Kolbitsch, Josef, and Hermann Maurer, "The Transformation of the Web: How Emerging Communities Shape the Information We Consume," *Journal of Universal Computer Science*, Vol. 12, No. 2, 2006, pp. 19–37.

Kolpack, Bryce D., "Assessment Center Approach to Police Officer Selection," *Police Chief*, Vol. 58, No. 9, September 1991, pp. 28–30, 44–46.

Kondrasuk, Jack N., "The Effects of 9/11 and Terrorism on Human Resource Management: Recovery, Reconsideration, and Renewal," *Employee Responsibilities and Rights Journal*, Vol. 16, No. 1, March 2004, pp. 25–35.

Koper, Christopher S., Edward R. Maguire, and Gretchen E. Moore, *Hiring and Retention Issues in Police Agencies: Readings on the Determinants of Police Strength, Hiring and Retention of Officers, and the Federal COPS Program*, Washington, D.C.: Urban Institute, October 2001. As of June 24, 2010: http://www.urban.org/UploadedPDF/410380_Hiring-and-Retention.pdf

Kowal, Julie, Bryan C. Hassel, and Emily Ayscue Hassel, *Financial Incentives for Hard-to-Staff Positions: Cross-Sector Lessons for Public Education*, Chicago, Ill.: Center for American Progress, November 2008. As of June 24, 2010: http://www.americanprogress.org/issues/2008/11/financial_incentives.html

Kraska, Peter B., "Militarization and Policing: Its Relevance to 21st Century Police," *Policing: A Journal of Policy and Practice*, Vol. 1, No. 4, 2007, pp. 501–513.

Kuruvila, Matthai, "80 Oakland Police Officers Get Layoff Notices," *San Francisco Chronicle*, June 29, 2010. As of July 2, 2010: http://articles.sfgate.com/2010-06-29/bay-area/21930012_1_police-union-police-groups-public-safety-program

Lachnit, Carroll, "Employee Referral Saves Time, Saves Money, Delivers Quality," *Workforce*, June 2001.

LaHuis, David M., "Individual Differences in Applicant Reactions: A Job-Search Perspective," *International Journal of Selection and Assessment*, Vol. 13, No. 2, June 2005, pp. 150–159.

Lambert, Eric, "The Impact of Organizational Justice on Correctional Staff," *Journal of Criminal Justice*, Vol. 31, No. 2, March–April 2003, pp. 155–168.

Lambert, Eric, and Nancy Hogan, "The Importance of Job Satisfaction and Organizational Commitment in Shaping Turnover Intent: A Test of a Causal Model," *Criminal Justice Review*, Vol. 34, No. 1, 2009, pp. 96–118.

Landy, Frank J., *Performance Appraisal in Police Departments*, Washington, D.C.: Police Foundation, 1977.

Langworthy, Robert H., Thomas Hughes, and Beth Sanders, *Law Enforcement Recruitment, Selection and Training: A Survey of Major Police Departments in the U.S.*, Highland Heights, Ky.: Academy of Criminal Justice Sciences, Police Section, 1995.

Lanier, Cathy, chief, Metropolitan Police Department, Washington, D.C., "Challenges of Police Recruiting in the District of Columbia," presentation, RAND Center for Quality Policing Recruitment and Retention Summit, Arlington, Va., June 2008. As of June 24, 2010:
http://www.cops.usdoj.gov/Default.asp?Item=2101#12

LAPD—*See* Los Angeles Police Department.

Larson, Richard C., *Police Deployment: New Tools for Planners*, Lexington, Mass.: Lexington Books, 1978.

Lavigna, Robert L., "Winning the War for Talent, Part II: Some Solutions," *Government Finance Review*, Vol. 21, No. 2, April 2005.

Lawler, Edward E. III, "Creating High Performance Organizations," *Asia Pacific Journal of Human Resources*, Vol. 4, No. 1, 2005, pp. 10–17.

Lawsson, Robert D., "Identifying and Managing Diversity of Workforce," *Business Intelligence Journal*, Vol. 2, No. 1, January 2009, pp. 215–253.

Lee, Christopher D., *Performance Conversations: An Alternative to Appraisals*, Tucson, Ariz.: Wheatmark, 2006.

Lee, Lori Ann, *Peace Officer Recruitment and Retention: Best Practices*, Sacramento, Calif.: Commission on Peace Officer Standards and Training, July 2001. As of June 23, 2010:
http://libcat.post.ca.gov/dbtw-wpd/documents/post/53936324.pdf

Lee, Thomas W., and Terence R. Mitchell, "An Alternative Approach: The Unfolding Model of Voluntary Employee Turnover," *Academy of Management Review*, Vol. 19, No. 1, January 1994, pp. 51–89.

Lee, Wendy, "LAPD May Relax Its Hiring Rules," *Los Angeles Times*, August 29, 2005. As of June 24, 2010:
http://articles.latimes.com/2005/aug/29/local/me-lapd29

Levenson, Michael, and Donovan Slack, "Pension Laws Pare Police, Fire Rolls," *Boston Globe*, July 1, 2009. As of June 24, 2010:
http://www.boston.com/news/local/massachusetts/articles/2009/07/01/pension_laws_pare_police_fire_rolls/

Levin-Epstein, Jodie, *Getting Punched: The Job and Family Clock*, Washington, D.C.: Center for Law and Social Policy, July 2006. As of June 24, 2010: http://www.clasp.org/admin/site/publications/files/0303.pdf

Lewis, Robert, "70 Deputies' Jobs Saved," *Sacramento Bee*, July 15, 2009. As of June 24, 2010: http://www.sacbee.com/2009/07/15/2026680/70-deputies-jobs-saved.html

Lewis, Suzan, Carolyn Kagan, and Patricia Heaton, "Managing Work-Family Diversity for Parents of Disabled Children: Beyond Policy to Practice and Partnership," *Personnel Review*, Vol. 29, No. 3, 2000, pp. 417–430.

Liebert, Dennis R., and Rod Miller, *Staffing Analysis Workbook for Jails*, Washington, D.C.: Department of Justice, National Institute of Corrections, 2001.

Lim, Nelson, Carl Matthies, Greg Ridgeway, and Brian Gifford, *To Protect and to Serve: Enhancing the Efficiency of LAPD Recruiting*, Santa Monica, Calif.: RAND Corporation, MG-881-RMPF, 2009. As of June 24, 2010: http://www.rand.org/pubs/monographs/MG881/

Litcher, Christopher D., Devon Reister, and Christopher Mason, *Statewide Law Enforcement Officer Retention Study*, Montpelier, Vt.: State of Vermont Law Enforcement Advisory Board, January 4, 2006. As of June 24, 2010: http://www.dps.state.vt.us/LEAB/law_enforcement_retention.pdf

Lloyd Morgan, *Driving Performance and Retention Through Employee Engagement*, undated. As of June 23, 2010: http://www.lloydmorgan.com/PDF/Driving%20Performance%20and%20 Retention%20Through%20Employee%20Engagement.pdf

London, Manuel, and Arthur J. Wohlers, "Agreement Between Subordinate and Self-Ratings in Upward Feedback," *Personnel Psychology*, Vol. 44, No. 2, Summer 1991, pp. 375–391.

Los Angeles Police Department, "To Protect and to Serve," undated video, webisode 1. As of June 24, 2010: http://www.joinlapd.com/webisode_01.html

Losey, Michael R., "Anticipating Change: Will There Be a Labor Shortage?" in Michael R. Losey, Susan R. Meisinger, and David Ulrich, eds., *The Future of Human Resource Management: 64 Thought Leaders Explore the Critical HR Issues of Today and Tomorrow*, Alexandria, Va.: Society for Human Resource Management, 2005, pp. 23–37.

Luthans, Kyle W., "Recognition: A Powerful, but Often Overlooked, Leadership Tool to Improve Employee Performance," *Journal of Leadership and Organizational Studies*, Vol. 7, No. 1, 2000, pp. 31–39.

Luthans, Kyle W., and Susan M. Jensen, "The Linkage Between Psychological Capital and Commitment to Organizational Mission: A Study of Nurses," *Journal of Nursing Administration*, Vol. 35, No. 6, June 2005, pp. 304–310.

Lynch, Jessica E., and Michelle Tuckey, *Understanding Voluntary Turnover: An Examination of Resignations in Australasian Police Organizations*, Payneham, Australia: Australasian Centre for Policing Research, report 143.1, 2004.

———, "The Police Turnover Problem: Fact or Fiction?" *Policing: An International Journal of Police Strategies and Management*, Vol. 31, No. 1, 2008, pp. 6–18.

Lyons, Sean, Linda Duxbury, and Chris Higgins, "An Empirical Assessment of Generational Differences in Work-Related Values," *Human Resources Management*, Vol. 26, No. 9, 2005, pp. 62–71.

Madrid, Ofelia, "Officer Applicants Surge at Scottsdale Police Department," *Arizona Republic*, March 26, 2009. As of June 24, 2010:
http://www.azcentral.com/news/articles/2009/03/26/20090326sr-pdrecruit0327.html

Maguire, Edward R., and Stephen D. Mastrofski, "Patterns of Community Policing in the United States," *Police Quarterly*, Vol. 3, No. 1, March 2000, pp. 4–45.

Maki, Amos, "Police Residency Tops Agenda," *Memphis Commercial-Appeal*, May 20, 2008. As of June 24, 2010:
http://www.commercialappeal.com/news/2008/may/20/police-residency-tops-agenda/

Makinen, Gail E., *The Economic Effects of 9/11: A Retrospective Assessment*, Washington, D.C.: Congressional Research Service, RL31617, September 27, 2002.

Manolatos, Tony, "S.D. Cops Flee City's Fiscal Mess, Seek Jobs at Other Departments," *San Diego Union-Tribune*, July 5, 2006. As of June 24, 2010:
http://legacy.signonsandiego.com/news/metro/20060705-9999-1n5gary.html

Martin, Graeme, Martin Reddington, and Mary Beth Kneafsey, *Web 2.0 and Human Resource Management: "Groundswell" or Hype?* London: Chartered Institute of Personnel and Development, 2009.

McCafferty, Francis L., "The Challenge of Selecting Tomorrow's Police Officers from Generations X and Y," *Journal of the American Academy of Psychiatry and the Law*, Vol. 31, No. 1, 2003, pp. 78–88.

McCoy, Mike, "Fire, Police Cuts Loom," *Santa Rosa Press-Democrat*, February 12, 2009. As of June 24, 2010:
http://www.pressdemocrat.com/article/20090212/NEWS/902120360

McDevitt, Jack, Amy Farrell, and Russell Wolf, *Promoting Cooperative Strategies to Reduce Racial Profiling*, Washington, D.C.: U.S. Department of Justice, Office of Community Oriented Policing Services, COPS evaluation brief 1, 2008. As of June 24, 2010:
http://purl.access.gpo.gov/GPO/LPS115585

McDonnell, Ken, "Benefit Cost Comparisons Between State and Local Governments and Private-Sector Employees," *Employee Benefit and Research Institute Notes*, Vol. 23, No. 10, October 2002, pp. 6–9.

———, "Benefit Cost Comparisons Between State and Local Governments and Private-Sector Employees," *Employee Benefit and Research Institute Notes*, Vol. 26, No. 4, April 2005, pp. 2–5.

———, "Benefit Cost Comparisons Between State and Local Governments and Private-Sector Employees," *Employee Benefit and Research Institute Notes*, Vol. 29, No. 6, June 2008, pp. 2–6.

McEvoy, Glenn M., and Wayne F. Cascio, "Do Good or Poor Performers Leave? A Meta-Analysis of the Relationship Between Performance and Turnover," *Academy of Management Journal*, Vol. 30, No. 4, December 1987, pp. 744–762.

McIntyre, Robert W., *Why Police Officers Resign: A Look at the Turnover of Police Officers in Vermont*, Montpelier, Vt.: Vermont Criminal Justice Center, 1990.

McKay, Patrick F., and Derek R. Avery, "Warning! Diversity Recruitment Could Backfire," *Journal of Management Inquiry*, Vol. 14, No. 4, December 2005, pp. 330–336.

———, "What Has Race Got to Do with It? Unraveling the Role of Racioethnicity in Job Seekers' Reactions to Site Visits," *Personnel Psychology*, Vol. 59, No. 2, Summer 2006, pp. 395–429.

McKeever, Jack, and April Kranda, "Recruitment and Retention of Qualified Police Personnel: A Best Practices Guide," *Big Ideas for Smaller Departments*, Vol. 2, No. 1, Summer 2000, pp. 3–15. As of June 24, 2010:
http://www.theiacp.org/LinkClick.aspx?fileticket=Jn02Pt%2BKiWI%3D&tabid=407

Meglino, Bruce M., Elizabeth C. Ravlin, and Angelo S. DeNisi, "A Meta-Analytic Examination of Realistic Job Preview Effectiveness: A Test of Three Counterintuitive Propositions," *Human Resource Management Review*, Vol. 10, No. 4, Winter 2000, pp. 407–434.

Meier, Gretl S., *Job Sharing: A New Pattern for Quality of Work and Life*, Kalamazoo, Mich.: W. E. Upjohn Institute for Employment Research, 1979.

Mestemaker, Michael J., *The Aviation Career Improvement Act and Its Impact on Retention*, Carlisle Barracks, Pa.: U.S. Army War College, 1991. As of June 24, 2010:
http://www.dtic.mil/cgi-bin/GetTRDoc?AD=ADA237336&Location=U2&doc=GetTRDoc.pdf

Metropolitan Atlanta Crime Commission, *Manual on Police Patrol Manpower Resource Allocation*, Atlanta, Ga., 1977.

Miller, Laura L., behavioral and social scientist, RAND Corporation, "Police Personnel Challenges After September 11: Anticipating Expanding Duties and a Changing Labor Pool," presentation, RAND Center for Quality Policing Recruitment and Retention Summit, Arlington, Va., June 2008. As of June 24, 2010:
http://www.cops.usdoj.gov/pdf/conference/rand/MillerPoliceChallengesafter911.pdf

Mitchell, Terence R., Brooks C. Holtom, Thomas W. Lee, and Ted Graske, "How to Keep Your Best Employees: Developing an Effective Retention Policy," *Academy of Management Executive (1993–2005)*, Vol. 15, No. 4, November 2001, pp. 96–109.

Mitchell, Terence R., Brooks C. Holtom, Thomas W. Lee, Chris J. Sablynski, and Miriam Erez, "Why People Stay: Using Job Embeddedness to Predict Voluntary Turnover," *Academy of Management Journal*, Vol. 44, No. 6, December 2001, pp. 1102–1121.

Mobley, William H., *Employee Turnover: Causes, Consequences, and Control*, Reading, Mass.: Addison-Wesley, 1982.

Moore, Solomon, "Despite Bleak Economy, Crime Numbers Take Positive Turn," *New York Times*, June 1, 2009. As of June 24, 2010:
http://www.nytimes.com/2009/06/02/us/02fbi.html

Morgan, Misti M., and William Allan Kritsonis, "A National Focus: The Recruitment, Retention, and Development of Quality Teachers in Hard-to-Staff Schools," *National Journal for Publishing and Mentoring Doctoral Student Research*, Vol. 5, No. 1, 2008, pp. 12–19.

Moriarty, Sean E., "The Leadership in Police Organizations Program in Delaware State Police: Recommendations for Law Enforcement Leadership Development," *Police Chief*, Vol. 76, No. 5, May 2009, pp. 7–13.

Moses, Joseph L., and Virginia R. Boehm, "Relationship of Assessment-Center Performance to Management Progress of Women," *Journal of Applied Psychology*, Vol. 60, No. 4, August 1975, pp. 527–529.

Moyle, Wendy, Jan Skinner, Gillian Rowe, and Chris Gork, "Views of Job Satisfaction and Dissatisfaction in Australian Long-Term Care," *Journal of Clinical Nursing*, Vol. 12, No. 2, March 2003, pp. 168–176.

Mueller, Charles W., and James L. Price, "Some Consequences of Turnover: A Work Unit Analysis," *Human Relations*, Vol. 42, No. 5, 1989, pp. 389–402.

Murphy, David W., and John L. Worrall, "Residency Requirements and Public Perceptions of the Police in Large Municipalities," *Policing: An International Journal of Police Strategies and Management*, Vol. 22, No. 3, 1999, pp. 327–342.

Musser, Linda R., "Effective Retention Strategies for Diverse Employees," *Journal of Library Administration*, Vol. 33, No. 1–2, January 2001, pp. 63–72.

"MySpace, Facebook and Other Social Networking Sites: Hot Today, Gone Tomorrow?" *Universia*, May 31, 2006. As of June 24, 2010:
http://www.wharton.universia.net/index.cfm?fa=viewfeature&id=1156&language=english

Nalla, Mahesh K., Michael Lynch, and Michael J. Leiber, "Determinants of Police Growth in Phoenix, 1950–1988," *Justice Quarterly*, Vol. 14, No. 1, March 1997, pp. 115–143.

Nash, James, and Elizabeth Gibson, "Supreme Court: Cities Can't Dictate Where Employees Live," *Columbus Dispatch*, June 10, 2009. As of June 24, 2010:
http://www.dispatch.com/live/content/local_news/stories/2009/06/10/asuprme.html

National Institute of Justice, *Assessing Criminal Justice Needs*, Washington, D.C., 1992.

New South Wales Council on the Cost of Government, *First Report*, Sydney, Australia, 1996.

New York City Commission to Combat Police Corruption, *Tenth Annual Report*, February 2008. As of June 24, 2010:
http://www.nyc.gov/html/ccpc/downloads/pdf/10th_annual_report_feb_2008.pdf

NIJ—*See* National Institute of Justice

"NYPD Facing a Flood of 20-and-Out Retirees," *Law Enforcement News: A Publication of John Jay College of Criminal Justice*, Vol. 26, No. 527, February 14, 2000. As of June 24, 2010:
http://www.lib.jjay.cuny.edu/len/2000/02.14/

O'Brien-Pallas, Linda, Christine Duffield, and Chris Alksnis, "Who Will Be There to Nurse? Retention of Nurses Nearing Retirement," *Journal of Nursing Administration*, Vol. 34, No. 6, June 2004, pp. 298–302.

Oettmeier, Timothy N., and Mary Ann Wycoff, *Personnel Performance Evaluations in the Community Policing Context*, Washington, D.C.: Police Executive Research Forum, July 1997.

OJP—*See* U.S. Department of Justice, Office of Justice Programs.

Olson, Roberta K., Margot Nelson, Carol Stuart, Linda Young, Ardelle Kleinsasser, Rose Schroedermeier, and Phyllis Newstrom, "Nursing Student Residency Program: A Model for Seamless Transition from Nursing Student to RN," *Journal of Nursing Administration*, Vol. 31, No. 1, January 2001, pp. 40–48.

Ontario Office of Fire Marshal, *Resource Book: The Application of Recruitment and Retention Principles*, 2006. As of June 24, 2010:
http://www.ofm.gov.on.ca/english/FireProtection/munguide/Volunteer%20Recruitment%20and%20Retention/default.asp

Orrick, W. Dwayne, "Calculating the Cost of Police Turnover," *Police Chief*, Vol. 69, No. 10, October 2002, pp. 100–103.

———, *Recruitment, Retention, and Turnover of Police Personnel: Reliable, Practical, and Effective Solutions*, Springfield, Ill.: Charles C. Thomas, 2008a.

———, "Maximizing Officer Retention," presentation, RAND Center for Quality Policing Recruitment and Retention Summit, Arlington, Va., June 2008b. As of June 24, 2010:
http://www.cops.usdoj.gov/Default.asp?Item=2101#11

Palmer, Jonathan, Cheri Speier, Michael Buckley, and Jo Ellen Moore, *Recruiting and Retaining IS Personnel: Factors Influencing Employee Turnover*, Boston, Mass.: Association for Computing Machinery Special Interest Group on Computer Personnel Research, 1998.

Patterson, Bernie L., "Job Experience and Perceived Job Stress Among Police, Correctional, and Probation/Parole Officers," *Criminal Justice and Behavior*, Vol. 19, No. 3, September 1992, pp. 260–285.

PCSO—*See* Pinal County Sheriff's Office.

Pennington, Karen, JoAnn G. Congdon, and Joan K. Magilvy, "Second-Career CNAs in Nursing Homes: Tapping an Underused Resource," *Journal of Gerontological Nursing*, Vol. 33, No. 6, June 2007, pp. 21–28.

Perrons, Diane, "Flexible Working and Equal Opportunities in the United Kingdom: A Case Study from Retail," *Environment and Planning*, Vol. 32, No. 10, 2000, pp. 1719–1734.

Pew Research Center for the People and the Press, *A Portrait of "Generation Next": How Young People View Their Lives, Futures and Politics*, Washington, D.C., January 2007. As of June 24, 2010:
http://people-press.org/reports/pdf/300.pdf

Phillips, Jean M., "Effects of Realistic Job Previews on Multiple Organizational Outcomes: A Meta-Analysis," *Academy of Management Journal*, Vol. 41, No. 6, December 1998, pp. 673–690.

Pierce, Jon L., and Randall B. Dunham, "The 12-Hour Work Day: A 48-Hour, Eight-Day Week," *Academy of Management Journal*, Vol. 35, No. 5, December 1992, pp. 1086–1098.

Piktialis, Diane, and Hal Morgan, "The Aging of the U.S. Workforce and Its Implications for Employers," *Compensation and Benefits Review*, Vol. 35, No. 1, 2003, pp. 57–63.

Pinal County Sheriff's Office, *Police Allocation Staffing Analysis*, Florence, Ariz., March 3, 2008. As of June 24, 2010:
http://pinalcountyaz.gov/Departments/Sheriff/AboutPCSO/Documents/FinalStaffingReportwithaddendums.pdf

Pitt, Leyland F., and B. Ramaseshan, "Realistic Job Information and Salesforce Turnover: An Investigative Study," *Journal of Managerial Psychology*, Vol. 10, No. 5, 1995, pp. 29–36.

Planty, Michael, Stephen Provasnik, William J. Hussar, Thomas D. Snyder, and Grace Kena, *The Condition of Education 2008*, Washington, D.C.: Claitors Publishing Division, June 2008. As of June 24, 2010:
http://nces.ed.gov/pubsearch/pubsinfo.asp?pubid=2008031

Plecki, Margaret L., Ana M. Elfers, and Michael S. Knapp, *Who's Teaching Washington's Children? What We Know—and What We Need to Know—About Teachers and the Quality of Teaching in the State*, Silverdale, Wash.: Center for Strengthening the Teaching Profession, University of Washington College of Education, August 2003. As of June 24, 2010:
http://depts.washington.edu/ctpmail/PDFs/WATeacherReport.pdf

Pomfret, John, "Police Finding It Hard to Fill Jobs," *Washington Post*, March 27, 2006. As of June 24, 2010:
http://www.washingtonpost.com/wp-dyn/content/article/2006/03/26/AR2006032600995.html

Poulson, Edward, captain, Oakland (Calif.) Police Department, presentation, RAND Center for Quality Policing Recruitment and Retention Summit, Arlington, Va., June 2008.

Presman, Dylan, Robert Chapman, and Linda Rosen, *Creative Partnerships: Supporting Youth, Building Communities*, Washington, D.C.: U.S. Department of Justice, Office of Community Oriented Policing Services, September 2002. As of June 24, 2010:
http://purl.access.gpo.gov/GPO/LPS24105

Prince, Heath J., *Retention and Advancement in the Retail Industry: A Career Ladder Approach*, Boston, Mass.: Jobs for the Future, August 2003. As of June 24, 2010:
http://www.jff.org/publications/workforce/retention-and-advancement-retail-industr/310

Pynes, Joan, and H. John Bernardin, "Entry-Level Police Selection: The Assessment Center Is an Alternative," *Journal of Criminal Justice*, Vol. 20, No. 1, 1992, pp. 41–52.

"Q & A Chief Bernard Melekian: Chief Looks Back as Tenure in City Nears Its End," *Pasadena Star-News*, October 18, 2009.

RAND Corporation, "Welcome to the Police Recruitment and Retention Clearinghouse," last updated June 25, 2010. As of June 25, 2010:
http://www.rand.org/ise/centers/quality_policing/cops/

Raymond, Barbara, Laura J. Hickman, Laura L. Miller, and Jennifer S. Wong, *Police Personnel Challenges After September 11: Anticipating Expanded Duties and a Changing Labor Pool*, Santa Monica, Calif.: RAND Corporation, OP-154-RC, 2005. As of June 24, 2010:
http://www.rand.org/pubs/occasional_papers/OP154/

Reiser, Martin, "Some Organizational Stresses on Policemen," *Journal of Police Science and Administration*, Vol. 2, No. 2, 1974, pp. 156–159.

Reuland, Melissa M., and John Stedman, *Recruitment and Selection for Community Policing: An Analysis of Organizational Change*, Washington, D.C.: Police Executive Research Forum, 1998.

Rice, Laura, "Navarre Speaks Out on Police Cuts," *Toledo on the Move*, April 23, 2009. As of June 24, 2010:
http://www.toledoonthemove.com/news/story.aspx?list=194900&id=291244

Rich, Motoko, "Factory Jobs Return, but Employers Find Skills Shortage," *New York Times*, July 1, 2010. As of July 2, 2010:
http://www.nytimes.com/2010/07/02/business/economy/02manufacturing.html

Richman, Amy L., Janet T. Civian, Laurie L. Shannon, E. Jeffrey Hill, and Robert T. Brennan, "The Relationship of Perceived Flexibility, Supportive Work-Life Policies, and Use of Formal Flexible Arrangements and Occasional Flexibility to Employee Engagement and Expected Retention," *Community, Work, and Family*, Vol. 11, No. 2, May 2008, pp. 183–197.

Ridgeway, Greg, Nelson Lim, Brian Gifford, Christopher Koper, Carl Matthies, Sara Hajiamiri, and Alexis Huynh, *Strategies for Improving Officer Recruitment in the San Diego Police Department*, Santa Monica, Calif.: RAND Corporation, MG-724-SDPD, 2008. As of June 24, 2010:
http://www.rand.org/pubs/monographs/MG724/

Riggio, Ronald E., Bronston T. Mayes, and Deidra J. Schleicher, "Using Assessment Center Methods for Measuring Undergraduate Student Business Outcomes," *Journal of Management Inquiry*, Vol. 12, No. 1, 2003, pp. 68–78.

Riley, K. Jack, Gregory F. Treverton, Jeremy M. Wilson, and Lois M. Davis, *State and Local Intelligence in the War on Terrorism*, Santa Monica, Calif.: RAND Corporation, MG-394-RC, 2005. As of June 24, 2010:
http://www.rand.org/pubs/monographs/MG394/

Riley, K. Jack, Susan Turner, John MacDonald, Greg Ridgeway, Terry L. Schell, Jeremy M. Wilson, Travis L. Dixon, Terry Fain, Dionne Barnes-Proby, and Brent D. Fulton, *Police-Community Relations in Cincinnati*, Santa Monica, Calif.: RAND Corporation, TR-333-CC, 2005. As of June 24, 2010: http://www.rand.org/pubs/technical_reports/TR333/

Riley, Warren, "New Orleans Experience," presentation, RAND Center for Quality Policing Recruitment and Retention Summit, Arlington, Va., June 2008.

Risher, Howard, "Planning a 'Next Generation' Salary System," *Compensation and Benefits Review*, Vol. 19, No. 2, 2002, pp. 13–22.

Roberg, Roy, and Scott Bonn, "Higher Education and Policing: Where Are We Now?" *Policing: An International Journal of Police Strategies and Management*, Vol. 27, No. 4, 2004, pp. 469–486.

Robinson, Sarah, Trevor Murrells, and Michael Clinton, "Highly Qualified and Highly Ambitious: Implications for Workforce Retention of Realising the Career Expectations of Graduate Nurses in England," *Human Resource Management Journal*, Vol. 16, No. 3, July 2006, pp. 287–312.

Rosenholtz, Susan J., "Career Ladders and Merit Pay: Capricious Fads or Fundamental Reforms?" *Elementary School Journal*, Vol. 86, No. 4, January 1986, pp. 513–529.

Ross, Joyce D., "Determination of the Predictive Validity of the Assessment Center Approach to Selecting Police Managers," *Journal of Criminal Justice*, Vol. 8, No. 2, 1980, pp. 89–96.

Rostker, Bernard D., William M. Hix, and Jeremy M. Wilson, *Recruitment and Retention: Lessons for the New Orleans Police Department*, Santa Monica, Calif.: RAND Corporation, MG-585-RC, 2007. As of June 24, 2010: http://www.rand.org/pubs/monographs/MG585/

Russell, Cristel Antonia, *Advertainment: Fusing Advertising and Entertainment*, Ann Arbor, Mich.: University of Michigan Yaffe Center for Persuasive Communication, 2007. As of June 24, 2010: http://www.bus.umich.edu/FacultyResearch/ResearchCenters/centers/Yaffe/downloads/Advertainment_teaching_materials.pdf

Rust, Roland T., Greg L. Stewart, Heather Miller, and Debbie Pielback, "The Satisfaction and Retention of Frontline Employees: A Customer Satisfaction Measurement Approach," *International Journal of Service Industry Management*, Vol. 7, No. 5, 1996, pp. 62–80.

Ryan, Ann Marie, S. David Kriska, Bradley J. West, and Joshua M. Sacco, "Anticipated Work/Family Conflict and Family Member Views: Role in Police Recruiting," *Policing: An International Journal of Police Strategies and Management*, Vol. 24, No. 2, 2001, pp. 228–239.

Rynes, Sara L., Robert D. Bretz Jr., and Barry A. Gerhart, "The Importance of Recruitment in Job Choice: A Different Way of Looking," *Personnel Psychology*, Vol. 44, No. 3, 1991, pp. 487–521.

Saari, Lise M., and Timothy A. Judge, "Employee Attitudes and Job Satisfaction," *Human Resource Management*, Vol. 43, No. 4, Winter 2004, pp. 395–407.

Sackett, Paul R., and Anne S. Mavor, *Attitudes, Aptitudes, and Aspirations of American Youth: Implications for Military Recruiting*, Washington, D.C.: National Academies Press, 2003.

Sánchez, Angel Martínez, Manuela Pérez Pérez, Pilar de Luis Carnicer, and Maria José Vela Jiménez, "Teleworking and Workplace Flexibility: A Study of Impact on Firm Performance," *Personnel Review*, Vol. 36, No. 1, 2007, pp. 42–64.

Sanders, Beth A., "Maybe There's No Such Thing as a 'Good Cop': Organizational Challenges in Selecting Quality Officers," *Policing: An International Journal of Police Strategies and* Management, Vol. 26, No. 2, 2003, pp. 313–328.

Sartain, Libby, and Mark Schumann, *Brand from the Inside: Eight Essentials to Emotionally Connect Your Employees to Your Business*, San Francisco, Calif.: Jossey-Bass Publishers, 2006.

Scheibe, John, "Applicants Seeking Stability of Police Gigs in Shaky Job Market," *Ventura County Star*, February 14, 2009. As of June 24, 2010: http://www.vcstar.com/news/2009/feb/14/well-at-least-somebodys-still-hiring-applicants/

Schein, Edgar, *Career Anchors: Discovering Your Real Values*, San Diego, Calif.: University Associates, 1990.

Schmidt, Michael S., "A Flood of Applicants to a Shrinking Police Dept.," *New York Times*, November 18, 2009. As of June 24, 2010: http://www.nytimes.com/2009/11/18/nyregion/18recruit.html

Scogin, Forest, Joseph Schumacher, Jennifer Gardner, and William Chaplin, "Predictive Validity of Psychological Testing in Law Enforcement Settings," *Professional Psychology: Research and Practice*, Vol. 26, No. 1, February 1995, pp. 68–71.

Scott, M. Douglas, chief, Arlington County (Va.) Police Department, "Competing in a Highly Competitive Job Market," presentation, RAND Center for Quality Policing Recruitment and Retention Summit, Arlington, Va., June 2008. As of June 24, 2010:
http://www.cops.usdoj.gov/pdf/conference/rand/ScottCompetinginaHighlyCompetitiveJobMarket.pdf

Scrivner, Ellen M., *Innovations in Police Recruitment and Hiring: Hiring in the Spirit of Service*, Washington, D.C.: U.S. Department of Justice, Office of Community Oriented Policing Services, January 26, 2006. As of June 24, 2010:
http://www.cops.usdoj.gov/ric/ResourceDetail.aspx?RID=113

———, "Recruitment and Hiring: Challenge or Opportunity for Change?" presentation, RAND Center for Quality Policing Recruitment and Retention Summit, Arlington, Va., June 2008. As of September 2, 2009: http://www.cops.usdoj.gov/pdf/conference/rand/ScrivnerRecruitmentpresentation.pdf

Searle, Rosalind H., "New Technology: The Potential Impact of Surveillance Techniques in Recruitment Practices," *Personnel Review*, Vol. 35, No. 3, 2006, pp. 336–351.

Seibert, Scott, "The Effectiveness of Facilitated Mentoring: A Longitudinal Quasi-Experiment," *Journal of Vocational Behavior*, Vol. 54, No. 3, June 1999, pp. 483–502.

Shane, Jon M., *What Every Chief Executive Should Know: Using Data to Measure Police Performance*, Flushing, N.Y.: Looseleaf Law Publications, 2007.

Shilling, Dana, *Retention Strategies for Key Employees in B-to-B Companies*, New York: American Business Media, 2004. As of June 24, 2010:
http://www.americanbusinessmedia.com/images/abm/pdfs/resources/Retention_Strategies.pdf

Sidener, Carrie J., "Lynchburg Police Department Sees Surge in Applications," *Lynchburg News and Advance*, May 6, 2009. As of June 24, 2010:
http://www2.newsadvance.com/lna/news/local/article/lynchburg_police_department_sees_surge_in_applications/15759/

Sigler, Kevin J., "Challenges of Employee Retention," *Management Research News*, Vol. 22, No. 10, 1999, pp. 1–6.

Skolnick, Jerome H., and David H. Bayley, "Theme and Variation in Community Policing," *Crime and Justice*, Vol. 10, 1988, pp. 1–37.

Slater, Harold R., and Martin Reiser, "Comparative Study of Factors Influencing Police Recruitment," *Journal of Police Science and Administration*, Vol. 16, No. 3, September 1988, pp. 168–176.

Smelson, I. Harold, "Psychiatric Screening of Police Candidates," *Journal of the Medical Society of New Jersey*, Vol. 72, No. 3, March 1975, pp. 213–216.

Smith, Thomas M., and Richard M. Ingersoll, "What Are the Effects of Induction and Mentoring on Beginning Teacher Turnover?" *American Educational Research Journal*, Vol. 41, No. 3, September 2004, pp. 681–714.

Sochalski, Julie, "Nursing Shortage Redux: Turning the Corner on an Enduring Problem," *Health Affairs*, Vol. 21, No. 5, 2002, pp. 157–164.

Sparger, Jerry R. and David J. Giacopassi, "Copping Out: Why Police Leave the Force," in Richard R. Bennett, ed., *Police at Work: Policy Issues and Analysis*, Thousand Oaks, Calif.: Sage Publications, 1983, pp. 107–124.

Sparks, Kate, Cary Cooper, Yitzhak Fried, and Arie Shirom, "The Effects of Hours of Work on Health: A Meta-Analytic Review," *Journal of Occupational and Organizational Psychology*, Vol. 70, No. 4, December 1997, pp. 391–408.

Spielman, Fran, "Early Retirement for Cops Helps Budget, Not Force," *Chicago Sun-Times*, July 23, 2009. As of June 24, 2010:
http://www.suntimes.com/news/cityhall/1681991,chicago-cops-shortage-retirement-072309.article

Spolar, Matthew, "Camden Acts to Change Police Residency Rule," *Philadelphia Inquirer*, September 9, 2009.

Spuck, Dennis W., "Reward Structures in the Public High School," *Educational Administration Quarterly*, Vol. 10, No. 1, January 1974, pp. 18–34.

Staiger, Douglas O., David I. Auerbach, and Peter I. Buerhaus, "Expanding Career Opportunities for Women and the Declining Interest in Nursing as a Career," *Nursing Economics*, Vol. 18, No. 5, September–October 2000, pp. 230–236.

Stairs, Martin, Martin Galpin, Nicky Page, and Alex Linley, "Retention on a Knife Edge: The Role of Employee Engagement in Talent Management," *Selection and Development Review*, Vol. 22, No. 95, 2006, pp. 19–23.

Stanley, Mary J., "How 'Ya Gonna Keep 'Em Down on the Farm: The Problem of Retention," *Indiana Libraries*, Vol. 27, No. 1, 2008, pp. 84–89.

Strawbridge, Peter, and Deirdre Strawbridge, *A Networking Guide to Recruitment, Selection and Probationary Training of Police Officers in Major Departments of the United States of America*, New York: John Jay College of Criminal Justice, 1990.

Sturm, Roland, Jeanne S. Ringel, Darius N. Lakdawalla, Jay Bhattacharya, Dana P. Goldman, Michael Hurd, Geoffrey F. Joyce, Constantijn Panis, and Tatiana Andreyeva, *Obesity and Disability: The Shape of Things to Come*, Santa Monica, Calif.: RAND Corporation, RB-9043-1, 2007. As of June 24, 2010: http://www.rand.org/pubs/research_briefs/RB9043-1/

Sullivan, John, "A Case Study of Google Recruiting," *Dr. John Sullivan's Talent Management Thought Leadership Community*, December 2005. As of June 24, 2010: http://www.drjohnsullivan.com/articles-mainmenu-27/hr-strategy-mainmenu-33/81-a-case-study-of-google-recruiting

Swanberg, Jennifer, "Job-Family Role Strain Among Low-Wage Workers," *Journal of Family and Economic Issues*, Vol 26, No. 1, March 2005, pp. 143–158.

Sward, Susan, "Newsom Likes Police Study, but Cash Is Tight," *San Francisco Chronicle*, November 3, 2008. As of June 24, 2010: http://articles.sfgate.com/2008-11-03/news/17129378_1_newsom-s-comments-new-officers-report-s-proposals

Switzer, Merlin E., *Recruitment and Retention: Best Practices Update*, Sacramento, Calif.: Commission on Peace Officer Standards and Training, April 2006.

Syrett, Michel, and Jean Lammiman, "Advertising and Millennials: Young Consumers," *Insight and Ideas for Responsible Marketers*, Vol. 5, No. 4, 2004, pp. 62–73.

Tadwalkar, Sunil, and Manjira Sen, "Manpower Retention in IT: An Oxymoron?" *Ubiquity*, Vol. 6, No. 14, April 26–May 3, 2005, pp. 2–13.

Taylor, Bruce, Bruce Kubu, Lorie Fridell, Carter Rees, Tom Jordan, and Jason Cheney, *Cop Crunch: Identifying Strategies for Dealing with the Recruiting and Hiring Crisis in Law Enforcement*, Washington, D.C.: Police Executive Research Forum, April 2006. As of June 24, 2010: http://www.ncjrs.gov/pdffiles1/nij/grants/213800.pdf

Tett, Robert P., and John P. Meyer, "Job Satisfaction, Organizational Commitment, Turnover Intention, and Turnover: Path Analyses Based on Meta-Analytic Findings," *Personnel Psychology*, Vol. 46, No. 2, December 2006, pp. 259–293.

Thibaut, John W., and Laurens Walker, *Procedural Justice: A Psychological Analysis*, Hillsdale, N.J.: L. Erlbaum Associates, 1975.

Tigchelaar, Anke, Niels Brouwer, and Jan D. Vermunt, "Tailor-Made: Towards a Pedagogy for Educating Second-Career Teachers," *Educational Research Review*, Vol. 5, No. 2, 2010, pp. 164–183.

Towers Perrin, *Working Today: Understanding What Drives Employee Engagement*, Stamford, Conn.: Towers Perrin, 2003. As of June 24, 2010:
http://www.towersperrin.com/tp/getwebcachedoc?webc=hrs/usa/2003/200309/talent_2003.pdf

Truxillo, Donald M., Dirk D. Steiner, and Stephen W. Gilliland, "The Importance of Organizational Justice in Personnel Selection: Defining When Selection Fairness Really Matters," *International Journal of Selection and Assessment*, Vol. 12, No. 1–2, March 2004, pp. 39–53.

Tsang, Eric W. K., and Shaker A. Zahra, "Organizational Unlearning," *Human Relations*, Vol. 61, No. 10, 2008, pp. 1435–1462.

Tulgan, Bruce, *Managing Generation X: How to Bring Out the Best in Young Talent*, Oxford: Capstone, 2000.

Tuomey, Lianne M., and Rachel Jolly, "Step Up to Law Enforcement: A Successful Strategy for Recruiting Women into the Law Enforcement Profession," *Police Chief*, Vol. 76, No. 6, June 2009, pp. 68–73.

Twenge, Jean M., and Stacy M. Campbell, "Generational Differences in Psychological Traits and Their Impact on the Workplace," *Journal of Managerial Psychology*, Vol. 23, No. 8, 2008, pp. 862–877.

U.S. Census Bureau, "U.S. Interim Projections by Age, Sex, Race, and Hispanic Origin: 2000–2050," undated website. As of June 24, 2010:
http://www.census.gov/population/www/projections/usinterimproj/

U.S. Department of Defense, Office of the Under Secretary of Defense for Personnel and Readiness, *Population Representation in the Military Services: Trends in Propensity*, Washington, D.C., March 2003.

U.S. Department of Education, Institute of Education Sciences, National Center for Education Statistics, *Digest of Education Statistics, 2005*, Washington, D.C., July 2006. As of June 24, 2010:
http://nces.ed.gov/pubsearch/pubsinfo.asp?pubid=2006030

U.S. Department of Justice, Office of Justice Programs, National Institute of Justice, *Policing in Arab-American Communities After September 11*, Washington, D.C., July 2008. As of June 24, 2010:
http://purl.access.gpo.gov/GPO/LPS103999

U.S. Department of Justice, Office of Community Oriented Policing Services, "2008 RAND Summit: Summit Proceedings," undated Web page (a). As of June 25, 2010:
http://www.cops.usdoj.gov/Default.asp?Item=2101

———, "About," undated Web page (b). As of June 24, 2010:
http://www.cops.usdoj.gov/Default.asp?Item=35

———, "COPS Hiring Recovery Program Update," *Community Policing Dispatch*, Vol. 2, No. 6, June 2009a. As of June 24, 2010:
http://www.cops.usdoj.gov/html/dispatch/June_2009/hiring_recovery.htm

———, *Law Enforcement Recruitment Toolkit*, Washington, D.C., October 16, 2009b. As of June 24, 2010:
http://www.cops.usdoj.gov/ric/ResourceDetail.aspx?RID=542

U.S. Department of Justice, Office of Justice Programs, Office of the Police Corps and Law Enforcement Education, *The Police Corps Annual Report to the President, the Attorney General, and the Congress*, Washington, D.C., 2003.

U.S. Department of State, *Trafficking in Persons Report 2009*, Washington, D.C., June 16, 2009. As of June 24, 2010:
http://www.state.gov/g/tip/rls/tiprpt/2009/index.htm

Van Hoye, Greet, and Filip Lievens, "Investigating Web-Based Recruitment Sources: Employee Testimonials vs. Word-of-Mouse," *International Journal of Selection and Assessment*, Vol. 15, No. 4, December 2007, pp. 372–382.

Verhoeven, Helen, Neelofer Mashood, and Bal Chansarkar, "Recruitment and Generation Y: Web 2.0 the Way to Go?" paper presented at the Annual American Business Research Conference, New York, N.Y., April 2009. As of June 24, 2010:
http://www.wbiconpro.com/8.Neelofar.pdf

Viney, Claire, Steve Adamson, and Noeleen Doherty, "Paradoxes of Fast-Track Career Management," *Personnel Review*, Vol. 26, No. 3, April 1997, pp. 174–186.

Violanti, John M., and Fred Aron, "Police Stressors: Variations in Perception Among Police Personnel," *Journal of Criminal Justice*, Vol. 23, No. 3, 1995, pp. 287–294.

Walker, Alan G., and James W. Smither, "A Five-Year Study of Upward Feedback: What Managers Do with Their Results Matters," *Personnel Psychology*, Vol. 52, No. 2, Summer 1999, pp. 393–423.

Walker, Samuel, ed., *Records of the Wickersham Commission on Law Observance and Enforcement*, Bethesda, Md.: University Publications of America, 1997.

———, *Police Accountability: Current Issues and Research Needs*, Washington, D.C.: U.S. Department of Justice, NCJ 218583, November 2006.

Webster, Barbara, and Edward F. Connors, *Police Chiefs and Sheriffs Rank Their Criminal Justice Needs*, Washington, D.C.: U.S. Department of Justice, National Institute of Justice, NCJ 113061, August 1988.

Wheeler, Christopher H., "Local Market Scale and the Pattern of Job Changes Among Young Men," *Regional Science and Urban Economics*, Vol. 38, No. 2, March 2008, pp. 101–118.

Whetstone, Thomas S., John C. Reed Jr., and Phillip C. Turner, "Recruiting: A Comparative Study of the Recruiting Practices of State Police Agencies," *International Journal of Police Science and Management*, Vol. 8, No. 1, Spring 2006, pp. 52–66.

White, Michael D., "Identifying Good Cops Early: Predicting Recruit Performance in the Academy," *Police Quarterly*, Vol. 11, No. 1, March 2008, pp. 27–49.

White, Michael D., and Gipsy Escobar, "Making Good Cops in the Twenty-First Century: Emerging Issues for the Effective Recruitment, Selection and Training of Police in the United States and Abroad," *Crime and Criminal Justice*, Vol. 22, No. 1–2, March 2008, pp. 119–134.

Wiegler, Laurie, "Big Brother in the Big Apple," *Engineering and Technology*, Vol. 3, No. 9, 2008, pp. 24–27.

Williams, Charles R., and Linda Parrack Livingstone, "Another Look at the Relationship Between Performance and Voluntary Turnover," *Academy of Management Journal*, Vol. 37, No. 2, April 1994, pp. 269–298.

Wilson, Jeremy M., *Community Policing in America*, New York: Routledge, 2006.

Wilson, Jeremy M., and Amy G. Cox, *Community Policing and Crime: The Process and Impact of Problem-Solving in Oakland*, Santa Monica, Calif.: RAND Corporation, TR-635-BPA, 2008. As of June 24, 2010: http://www.rand.org/pubs/technical_reports/TR635/

Wilson, Jeremy M., Amy G. Cox, Tommy L. Smith, Hans Bos, and Terry Fain, *Community Policing and Violence Prevention in Oakland: Measure Y in Action*, Santa Monica, Calif.: RAND Corporation, TR-546-BPA, 2007. As of June 24, 2010: http://www.rand.org/pubs/technical_reports/TR546/

Wilson, Jeremy M., and Clifford A. Grammich, *Police Recruitment and Retention in the Contemporary Urban Environment: A National Discussion of Personnel Experiences and Promising Practices from the Front Lines*, Santa Monica, Calif.: RAND Corporation, CF-261-DOJ, 2009a. As of June 24, 2010: http://www.rand.org/pubs/conf_proceedings/CF261/

———, "Reconstructing Internal Security in Post-Conflict Societies: The Challenge and Successfulness of Developing Democratic Police and Justice Institutions," *Security Journal*, June 22, 2009b.

Wilson, Jeremy M., Bernard D. Rostker, and Mike Hix, "Police Recruitment and Retention in New Orleans: Crisis as Catalyst," presentation, RAND Center for Quality Policing Recruitment and Retention Summit, Arlington, Va., June 2008. As of June 24, 2010: http://www.cops.usdoj.gov/pdf/conference/rand/WilsonPoliceRecruitmentNO.pdf

Wilson, Michael J., James B. Greenlee, Tracey Hagerty, Cynthia v. Helba, D. Wayne Hintze, and Jerome D. Lehnus, *Youth Attitude Tracking Study: 1999 Propensity and Advertising Report*, Arlington, Va.: Defense Manpower Data Center, June 14, 2000. As of June 24, 2010: http://handle.dtic.mil/100.2/ADA385236

Winston, Ali, "The Eyes Have It: NYPD Plans More Cameras," *City Limits*, June 1, 2009. As of June 24, 2010: http://www.citylimits.org/news/articles/3751/the-eyes-have-it

Wolf, Andrea, and Sarah Rohrs, "Fire and Police Retirement Papers Flooding In," *Vallejo (Calif.) Times Herald*, February 15, 2008.

Womack, Amy Leigh, "Plan Might Cause Police, Fire Exodus," *Macon Sun News*, June 6, 2009. As of June 24, 2010: http://www.macon.com/2009/06/06/739315/plan-might-cause-police-fire-exodus.html

Woska, William J., "Police Officer Recruitment: A Public-Sector Crisis," *Police Chief*, Vol. 73, No. 10, October 2006, pp. 52–59.

Wright, Jerome, "Adding to Police Ranks Rankles," *Memphis Commercial Appeal*, February 1, 2009. As of June 24, 2010: http://www.commercialappeal.com/news/2009/feb/01/adding-to-ranks-rankles/

Yearwood, Douglas L., *Recruitment and Retention Study Series: Sworn Sheriffs' Personnel*, Raleigh, N.C.: North Carolina Sheriffs' Education and Training Standards Commission, April 2003. As of June 24, 2010: http://www.ncgccd.org/PDFs/Pubs/NCCJAC/rrsheriff.pdf

Yearwood, Douglas L., and Stephanie Freeman, "Analyzing Concerns Among Police Admnistrators: Recruitment and Retention of Police Officers in North Carolina," *Police Chief*, Vol. 71, No. 3, March 2004, pp. 43–49.

Zhao, Jihong, Nicholas P. Lovrich, and Quint Thurman, "The Status of Community Policing in American Cities: Facilitators and Impediments Revised," *Policing: An International Journal of Police Strategies and Management*, Vol. 22, No. 1, 1999, pp. 74–92.